TRADITIONAL
TWO BLOCK
QUILTS

Sally Saulmon

American Quilter's Society
P. O. Box 3290 • Paducah, KY 42002-3290
www.AmericanQuilter.com

Located in Paducah, Kentucky, the American Quilter's Society (AQS) is dedicated to promoting the accomplishments of today's quilters. Through its publications and events, AQS strives to honor today's quiltmakers and their work and to inspire future creativity and innovation in quiltmaking.

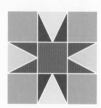

EDITOR: BARBARA SMITH
GRAPHIC DESIGN: ELAINE WILSON
COVER DESIGN: MICHAEL BUCKINGHAM
PHOTOGRAPHY: CHARLES R. LYNCH

Library of Congress Cataloging-in-Publication Data
Saulmon, Sally
    Traditional two block quilts / by Sally Saulmon.
        p. cm.
    Summary: "Design tips for making two-block traditional quilts. Fourteen patterns provided for machine piecing. Measurements provided for rotary cutting pieces and patterns for odd-sized pieces and appliques"--Provided by publisher.
    ISBN 1-57432-886-7
    1. Patchwork--Patterns. 2. Machine quilting--Patterns. I. Title.

TT835.S268 2005
746.46'041--dc22

                2005018199

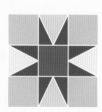

Additional copies of this book may be ordered from the American Quilter's Society, PO Box 3290, Paducah, KY 42002-3290; 800-626-5420 (orders only please); or online at www.AmericanQuilter.com. For all other inquiries, call 270-898-7903.

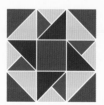

Acknowledgments

Thanks to the staff at American Quilter's Society for their encouragement, help, and professionalism. My editor, Barbara Smith, has been wonderful to work with.

My quilting friends, Terri Lynn Ballard and Nancy Grove, are always there with encouragement and applause for my efforts at creativity. The ideas they share spur me on to further endeavors. To Judy Case, thank you for your inspired machine-quilting designs on five of the quilts in this book. Without you, deadlines could not have been met.

To Caitlin and Wyatt, you have given me the unexpected joy of being your "Grammy." I had no idea that being a grandmother could tug at my heart so strongly. To Jenni, I'm forever grateful that you came into our lives to complete our family and bring us such delight. To Mike, you have enriched my life beyond belief, and I haven't been the same since that first day of motherhood. As always, with love to Bob, thanks for our 47 years of life together. Without you and the kids, I would just be an old lady knee-deep in quilts. Instead, I'm knee-deep in hoopla!

WORLD WITHOUT END, *by the author*

Contents

Introduction

Combining two or more different block patterns in the same quilt is not a new concept. The Double Irish Chain and the Snowball quilts are familiar combinations of traditional blocks. In Barbara Brackman's *An Encyclopedia of Pieced Quilt Patterns*, a number of two- and three-block patterns are attributed to quilt designers and publications of the past, including Nancy Cabot, Ruby McKim, Mrs. Danner, Aunt Martha, *Kansas City Star*, *Progressive Farmer*, *Capper's*, and *Farm Journal*. The most common set for these traditional combinations was the alternating of the blocks checkerboard style. Now, contemporary quiltmakers have discovered that combining two or more traditional or original block patterns is a great design technique to start on the road to creativity.

Multi-block quilts often produce interesting secondary patterns and illusions. When blocks containing 30- and 60-degree angles connect with blocks containing 45- and 90-degree angles, secondary circular patterns appear from straight lines. The illusion of sashing appears when combining a cross or X block with a second block. The rotation of directional blocks reveals strong secondary patterns. Combining more than two blocks or combining a pieced block with an appliquéd block can take this design even further. Fabric and color selection can enhance the patterns to produce illusions and interlocking designs, and the choice of an innovative setting that combines blocks can produce striking results.

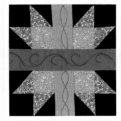

On the following pages, you will find guidelines and techniques for designing and making this type of quilt. Included are 14 quilt patterns for your use. I hope you will try these design ideas and enjoy the experience of creating a quilt that is uniquely yours.

Playing with Blocks

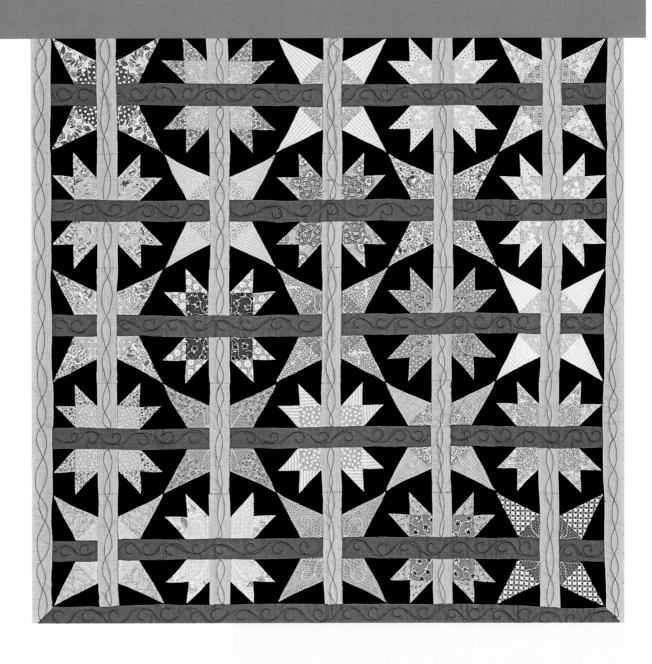

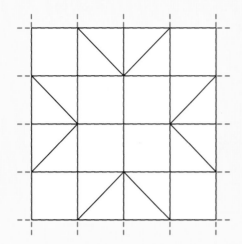

Fig. 1. *Sawtooth Star, four-patch grid*

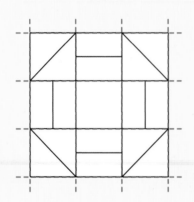

Fig. 2. *Churn Dash, nine-patch block*

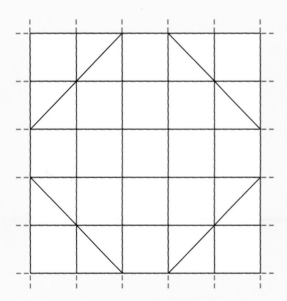

Fig. 3. *Double Wrench, five-patch grid*

CLASSIFICATION OF BLOCKS

Most traditional quilt designs fit into a grid or a classification, depending on the divisions in the block. For instance, the traditional Sawtooth Star falls into the four-patch category because it can be divided into four equal divisions across the top (fig. 1). A familiar nine-patch design is the Churn Dash, as shown in figure 2. (The nine-patch block is an exception because it is named for the total number of grid sections instead of the number of divisions across the top.) The Double Wrench is a five-patch grid design because it has five divisions across the top (fig. 3).

Other classifications include seven-patch designs and those based on an eight-pointed star or six-pointed star. When beginning to design quilts that combine more than one block pattern, success comes easily by combining blocks from the same classification. After you have some experience, it is fun to experiment by combining blocks from different classifications. For example, a six-inch four-patch and a six-inch nine-patch may produce an innovative result (fig. 4).

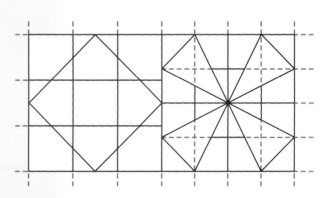

Fig. 4. *Combining blocks with different grids*

COMBINING TWO BLOCKS

The complexity of the blocks being combined should be considered. A combination may look dynamite on paper, but can it be constructed from fabric with some degree of ease? The degree of difficulty rises quickly when more than five patches meet at an intersection.

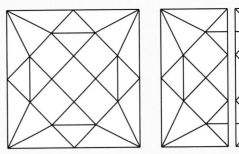

FIG. 5. *Symmetrical block*

Asymmetrical Blocks

Blocks used in quiltmaking are either symmetrical or asymmetrical. If a line is drawn down the middle of a symmetrical block, the two sides will be mirror images (fig. 5). In an asymmetrical (also called "directional") block, the two sides will be different and the four corners will also be different (fig. 6). A symmetrical block can become directional with the use of different fabrics in similar patches (fig. 7).

Asymmetrical blocks can maintain the same position or direction throughout a quilt or they can be rotated. TEMPO (photo 1) is an example of a quilt that combines two asymmetrical blocks. Block 1 maintains the same direction throughout the quilt, but block 2 is rotated. Strong secondary patterns are revealed in this quilt because of the positioning of the directional blocks.

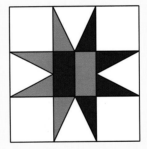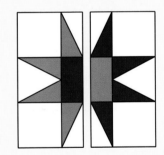

FIG. 6. *Directional block*

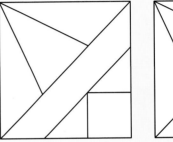

FIG. 7. *Fabric placement can make a symmetrical block into a directional one.*

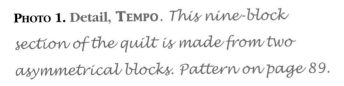

PHOTO 1. Detail, TEMPO. *This nine-block section of the quilt is made from two asymmetrical blocks. Pattern on page 89.*

PHOTO 2. Detail, MOONGLOW. *Blocks rotate first one way then the other. Pattern on page 58.*

Another example of rotation is shown in MOONGLOW (photo 2). The blocks in this quilt were not rotated 360 degrees as in TEMPO but were rotated only 90 degrees to reveal the pattern. Other examples of quilts that have 360-degree rotating blocks include STARSTRUCK (photo 3) and HOOPLA (photo 4).

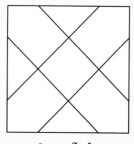

PHOTO 4. Detail, HOOPLA. *Rotating block 2 creates star points. Pattern on page 53.*

PHOTO 3. Detail, STARSTRUCK. *Block 2 rotates around a star block. Pattern on page 83.*

X BLOCKS

Snowflake

Nine X

CROSS BLOCKS

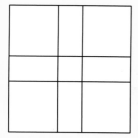

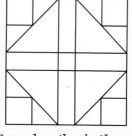

Unequal Nine Patch

Grandmother's Choice

FIG. 8.

The Illusion of Sashing

When an X block or a cross block is combined with another block, the illusion of sashing appears. Some common X blocks and cross blocks are shown in figure 8. The X block in AROUND THE BLOCK (photo 5) provides the illusion of sashing for the traditional Courthouse Steps block. In RETRO ROCKETS (photo 6), the crosses in both blocks 1 and 2 create the illusion of a woven sashing. The sashing illusion then encompasses a secondary directional block.

PHOTO 5. Detail, AROUND THE BLOCK. *X blocks create the appearance of sashing. Pattern on page 22.*

PHOTO 6. Detail, RETRO ROCKETS. *These cross blocks create woven sashing. Pattern on page 77.*

The Illusion of Circles

Angles of 30 and 60 degrees connected with 45- and 90-degree angles create the illusion of circles even though the lines are straight. In photo 7, a 60-degree angle connects with a 45-degree angle to produce the illusion of a circle. The distribution of color enhances the effect.

WORLD WITHOUT END (photo 8) is an example of 45- and 90-degree angles connecting with 30- and 60-degree angles. In RETRO ROCKETS (photo 9), with the black background used in both block 1 and block 2 and the 30-degree points of block 1 touching in the corners, the illusion of curved lines is produced.

PHOTO 7. *This block appears to have curves.*

PHOTO 8. Detail, WORLD WITHOUT END. *Connecting a 30-degree and a 45-degree angle also produces a curved effect. Pattern on page 95.*

PHOTO 9. Detail, RETRO ROCKETS. *Another example of the illusion of curves. Pattern on page 77.*

PHOTO 10. Detail, PERSIAN PUZZLE. *Original block designs are lost when combined. Pattern on page 71.*

PHOTO 11. Detail, AROUND THE BLOCK. *The use of light and dark fabrics hides the block seam lines. Pattern on page 22.*

PHOTO 12. Detail, STARSTRUCK. *There are only two blocks, but fabric selection creates interlocking patterns. Pattern on page 83.*

Value and Intensity

Fabrics and their value and intensity can be used to blur the seam lines where blocks are combined. The patterns then seem to interlock and flow together. The results are unexpected secondary patterns. PERSIAN PUZZLE (photo 10) is an example of how the original block designs are lost when combined. By the use of beige fabric in adjoining pieces, the seam lines become diffused. In both block 1 and block 2, the four corner triangles are cut from striped fabric. This further buries the seam lines.

The placement of light and dark fabrics in AROUND THE BLOCK (photo 11) obliterates the seam lines between the blocks. The result is the appearance of a Log Cabin variation set on point with sashing. STARSTRUCK (photo 12) is another quilt with interlocking patterns produced by fabric selection.

Other Block Shapes

Blocks do not have to be square. When rectangular blocks are combined, surprising results are produced. PERSIAN PUZZLE (photo 13) is an example of an experiment with rectangular blocks.

PHOTO 13. Detail, PERSIAN PUZZLE. *This seemingly elaborate design is made with only two rectangular blocks. Pattern on page 71.*

PHOTO 14. Detail, *XANADU. A three-block quilt. Pattern on page 103.*

COMBINING THREE BLOCKS

The concept of combining blocks to produce secondary patterns is not limited to just two traditional blocks. Three blocks have been combined in XANADU then set on point (photo 14). By maintaining the value in pieces that are adjoining, strong secondary patterns emerge.

By having a consistent background fabric in the three blocks of CENTENNIAL MEDALLION (photo 15), the adjacent seam lines are lost. The three blocks interweave to form a medallion.

PHOTO 15. Detail, CENTENNIAL MEDALLION. *A consistent background fabric ties the blocks together. Pattern on page 34.*

COMBINING PATCHWORK AND APPLIQUÉ

The simplest of block combinations are enhanced with appliqué. In MOTHER'S KITCHEN (photo 16), a checkerboard block is alternated with a rotating appliqué block. By adding patchwork to the appliqué, secondary patterns are given movement. The repetition of an appliqué vine produces a trellis effect, as in COUNTRY ROAD (photo 17).

PHOTO 16. Detail, MOTHER'S KITCHEN. *Pattern on page 65.*

PHOTO 17. Detail, COUNTRY ROAD. *Pattern on page 41.*

Set Variations

FIG. 9. *Checkerboard set*

CHECKERBOARD SET

The usual set for quilts containing more than one block is the checkerboard pattern (fig. 9). Most of the patterns in this book are set in the traditional checkerboard arrangement.

DIAGONAL SET

Another option is to set the blocks diagonally on point. Diagonal sets require setting triangles around the perimeter to square off the quilt (fig. 10). Some blocks are more interesting when set on point, such as GARDEN MAZE (photo 18). By setting the blocks on point in a checkerboard pattern, 16 of block 1 and only nine of block 2 were required. Setting triangles can be plain or pieced. The setting triangles in XANADU (photo 19) are pieced to further extend the secondary pattern.

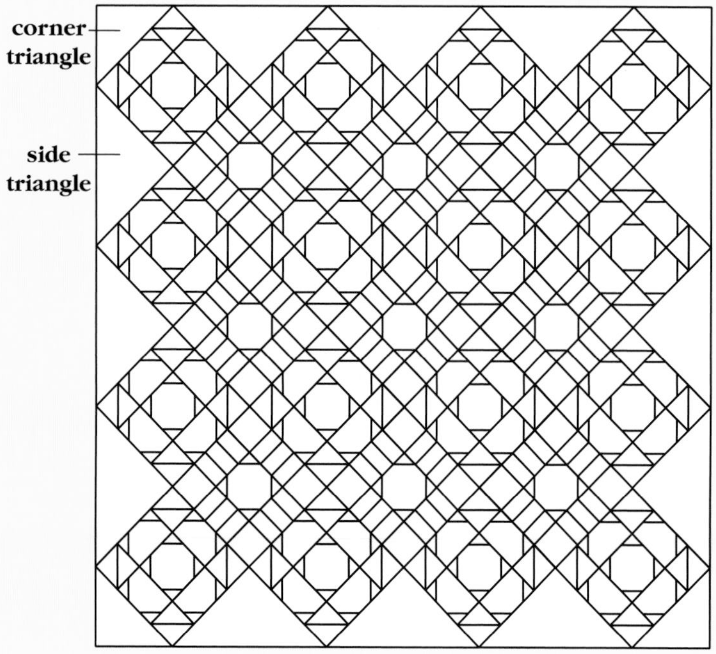

corner
triangle

side
triangle

FIG. 10. *Diagonal set*

PHOTO 18. Detail, GARDEN MAZE. *Pattern on page 47.*

SASHING

In MOONGLOW (photo 20), depth is achieved by separating the blocks with a narrow sashing. Another traditional set that can be used with two-block quilts is a strippy set. By using only vertical sashing, a traditional feeling is given to a contemporary design. BOUNTIFUL BASKETS (photo 21) has that traditional feel.

PHOTO 19. Detail, XANADU.
Pattern on page 103.

PHOTO 20. Detail, MOONGLOW. *Pattern on page 58.*

PHOTO 21. Detail, BOUNTIFUL BASKETS. *Pattern on page 28.*

Sally Saulmon • TRADITIONAL Two Block Quilts •

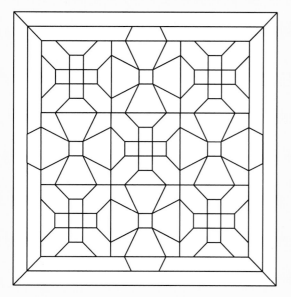

FIG. 11. *Block design extends into inner border.*

BORDERS

Borders frame a quilt. Most quilts do not appear to be finished without a border. However, in some geometric quilts, borders stop the design too soon. Designs that are extended into the borders alleviate this unfinished feeling. Figure 11 shows how extending part of the design into the border completes the pattern. An ethereal quality is achieved in WORLD WITHOUT END (photo 22) by extending the pattern into a print border.

PHOTO 22. Detail, WORLD WITHOUT END. *Pattern on page 95. Design extends into border.*

Beginning Design

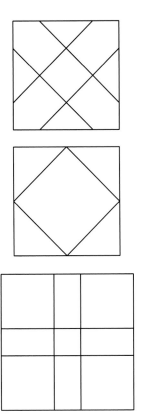

FIG. 12. *These simple blocks can be combined with more complex blocks.*

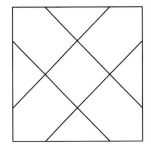 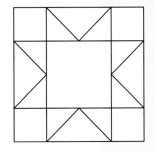

FIG. 13. *A basic X block and a star block*

In the pattern section of this book, there are 14 two- or three-block quilts with complete instructions for your use. However, if you would like to design a combination quilt of your own, the following ideas may help.

Good designs happen from a lot of experimenting. The experimental process can be expedited by using a quilt design software program on your computer. The whole layout can be set up on a grid: the blocks can be interspersed, changed, deleted, rotated, colored, and shaded; fabric motifs inserted; patterns for the quilt made and printed; and yardages calculated. For those so inclined, the computer is a wonderful tool.

Personally, I spend a lot of time on the computer figuring out the process instead of focusing on the design. Ideas come to me at all times of the day and night and not necessarily when I'm at the computer. Occasionally, my designs look professional right out of the computer, but more often, they are on scraps of paper or napkins, then hand-drawn on ¼" graph paper colored with pencils, crayons, or whatever my grandchildren have not pirated away. The important thing is to be comfortable with your design process.

After reviewing the ideas presented in the Playing with Blocks (page 7) and Set Variations (page 14) sections of this book, experiment by combining a simple block (fig.12) with a more complex block. Any of the basic blocks can be combined with a star block to produce a simple, but effective combination. See figure 13 for an example. Once the design seems appropriate,

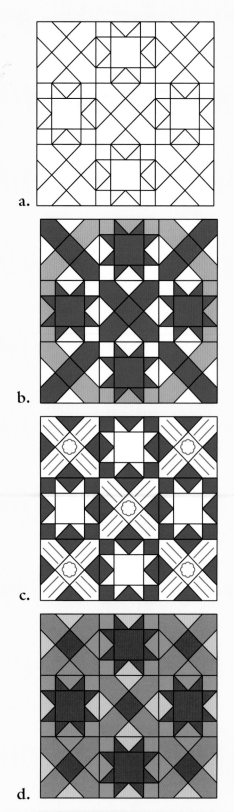

FIG. 14. *Effect of value on a two-block pattern: (a) basic pattern, (b) dark stars, (c) light stars with stripe in X blocks, (d) varied background.*

decide what part should dominate or be emphasized. Consider how light and dark values relate to those in adjacent blocks. Make copies of your favorite designs and shade in or color them in different ways.

Figure 14 shows examples of different colorations and shadings of a design composed of star and X blocks. In one example, the stars are dark, in another they are light, and in the third the background colors are varied. Begin to think about what fabrics to use. Figure 14c indicates that a striped or directional fabric might create the illusion of sashing. More important than the design of the fabrics are the values and intensities of the fabrics. When designing, ask yourself questions, such as, "Should any of the pieces be selectively cut from a medium to large print fabric? Can scraps be used effectively, or would a minimal number of fabrics be more striking?"

The experimental process can continue by choosing a more complicated set of blocks. Perhaps combining blocks that contain more complex angles will produce a design that yields unexpected secondary patterns. If a design becomes too intricate, erase some of the lines to simplify it.

There are way too many possible designs out there for all to be interpreted into a finished quilt. Several things have to come together to work into a completed project. An intriguing design is the beginning, but it has to be represented in fabric. A good design needs to be challenging yet relatively easy to construct. The fabrics chosen should be appropriate in scale, intensity, and design to implement the plan of the quilt. And, finally, the product should be worthy of the process. Have fun!

Project Tips

STRIPED FABRIC

When purchasing striped fabric, the amount needed depends on the number of repeats of the stripe across the width of the fabric. Large border-type stripes will usually repeat four or five times across the width, but a small stripe may repeat as many as 20 times. The fabric requirements for a stripe in the appropriate patterns are given in running inches by a certain width. This indicates the amount needed of a certain stripe motif. So, if the stripe is repeated 10 times across the width of the fabric, divide the running inches by 10 to find the yardage. For example, if the pattern calls for 540 running inches and your fabric has 10 repeats across the width, divide 540 by the 10 repeats to arrive at 54" or 1½ yards of fabric.

Before measuring and cutting your fabric, wash, dry, and iron it to ensure that the fabric will not bleed excess dye or shrink after the quilt is completed. Selvages have a tendency to pucker, so they should be removed.

CUTTING

Plan to cut larger pattern pieces, binding, and border strips first when cutting from a large piece of fabric. For the optimal use of the fabric, the edges of templates should be touching.

Rotary cutting dimensions, where applicable, are given in the cutting list for each pattern. The dimensions for rotary cutting include seam allowances.

Full-sized templates are provided for pieces that cannot be easily cut with a rotary cutter. If only half of the pattern piece is given, place the dotted line on the fold of the fabric. Where two halves of an asymmetrical pattern piece are given, join the template on the dashed line. Templates show both a seam line and a cutting line.

If a pattern letter is followed by an "r," this indicates that the template must be turned over before being traced on the fabric. Then you can cut the appropriate number of reversed pieces.

Appliqué templates do not include seam allowances. Depending on your favorite method of appliqué, add the necessary turn-under allowance to the pattern when cutting out the fabric patches. For the stems in the appliqué patterns, cut a bias strip 1¼" wide and fold it in half lengthwise, right side out. Sew ¼" from the fold then trim away the excess allowance. Press the strip so that the seam is hidden on the back of the stem.

SEWING AND PRESSING

One-fourth inch seam allowances are used for these patterns. If you do not have an accurate presser foot to follow, place a strip of masking tape ¼" away from the needle for a seam allowance guide.

Seam allowances should be pressed to one side, depending on the ease of construction or, if possible, toward the darker fabrics. The illustrations showing block construction have arrows indicating the direction for pressing seam allowances where it's important for joining seams. Use caution when pressing to avoid distorting seams and bias edges.

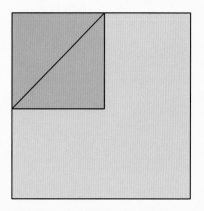

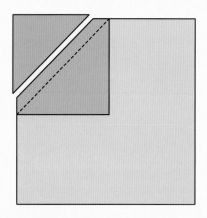

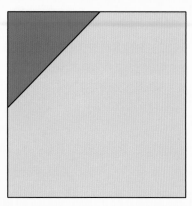

FIG. 15. *Corner-square technique*

CORNER-SQUARE TECHNIQUE

With this technique, you can easily add triangle corners to rectangles and squares, without having to handle those tiny triangles (fig. 15). As a disadvantage, the corner-square technique uses more fabric.

1. Draw a diagonal line, corner to corner, on the wrong side of a square. Align the square in the corner of a larger rectangle or square, right sides together.

2. Sew along the drawn line. Cut off the extra fabric in the corner, leaving a ¼" seam allowance.

3. Press the triangle open.

Important – Squares sized for the corner-square technique are not large enough to use for making half-square triangles. If you prefer to use half-square triangles in place of the corner-square technique, add another ⅜" to the size of the rotary-cut square. For example, a 2" (short side) finished triangle needs to start as a 2½" square for the corner-square technique. But for a half-square triangle that finishes 2", the starting square needs to be 2⅞".

Quilt Patterns

⬜ = Cut square diagonally.

⬜ = Cut square in quarters.

⬜ = See Corner-Square Technique, page 20.

r = reversed pattern

↑ = Arrows in figures indicate seam allowance pressing.

Around the Block

Fabric Requirements

Yardage is based on 40" wide fabric.

Fabric	Amount
Gold print	¼ yd
Brown stripe	550 running inches by 2" wide. See Striped Fabric, page 19, for determining yardage.
Lights – beiges & tans	1¼ yd total
Darks – browns, blacks & madder reds	1¼ yd total
Large brown print	1⅞ yd
Backing	3 yd (2 panels 33" x 50")
Batting	50" x 64"
Binding	½ yd (6 strips 2½" x 40")

Making Blocks

Patterns are on page 27.

BLOCK 1

BLOCK 2

• TRADITIONAL **Two Block Quilts** • Sally Saulmon

AROUND THE BLOCK, *by the author. Alternating a traditional Courthouse Steps block and an X block with light and dark colors produces the illusion of sashing. Civil War reproduction fabrics were used in this quilt to maintain an antique look.*

Fabric	Cutting
Gold print	18 pattern A
Brown stripe	72 pattern B
Lights – beiges & tans	12 strips 1¼" x 40", sewn in sets of 3. Use pattern C to cut the 4 strip-sets into 36 C triangles.
Darks – browns, blacks & madder reds	12 strips 1¼" x 40", sewn in sets of 3. Use pattern C to cut the 4 strip-sets into 36 C triangles.

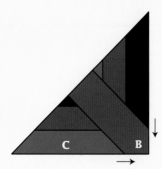

FIG. 16

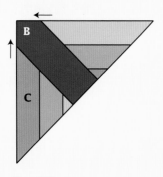

FIG. 17

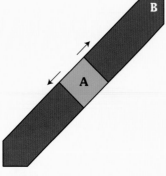

FIG. 18

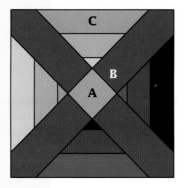

FIG. 19

Block 1 Assembly

1. Sew a dark C triangle to each side of a striped B (fig. 16). Make 18 units.

2. Sew a light C triangle to each side of a striped B (fig. 17). Make 18 units.

3. Sew a striped B to each side of a gold A square (fig. 18). Make 18 units.

4. Join the units as shown in figure 19 to complete the block. Make 18 of block 1.

Fabric	Cutting
Gold print	17 D squares 1½" x 1½"
Lights – beiges & tans	17 squares 1½" x 1½" (patch 2)
	34 rectangles 1½" x 3½" (patches 4 & 6)
	34 rectangles 1½" x 5½" (patches 8 & 10)
	17 rectangles 1½" x 7½" (patch 12)
Darks – browns, blacks & madder reds	17 squares 1½" x 1½" (patch 1)
	34 rectangles 1½" x 3½" (patches 3 & 5)
	34 rectangles 1½" x 5½" (patches 7 & 9)
	17 rectangles 1½" x 7½" (patch 11)

Block 2 Assembly

1. Sew a dark patch 1 to the left side of a gold D square. Sew a light patch 2 to the right side of a gold D square (fig. 20).

2. Continue to add patches 3–12 in numerical order to complete the block. Press all seam allowances away from the D square (fig. 21). Make 17 of block 2.

Fig. 20

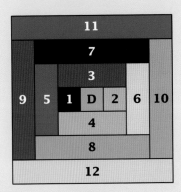

Fig. 21

Border Cutting

Border lengths include 2½" extra for insurance and seam allowances.

Fabric	Cutting
Brown stripe	2 strips 2" x 40½", top and bottom inner borders
	2 strips 2" x 54½", side inner borders
Large brown print (Cut strips parallel to selvages.)	2 strips 4½" x 48½", top and bottom outer borders
	2 strips 4½" x 62½", side inner borders

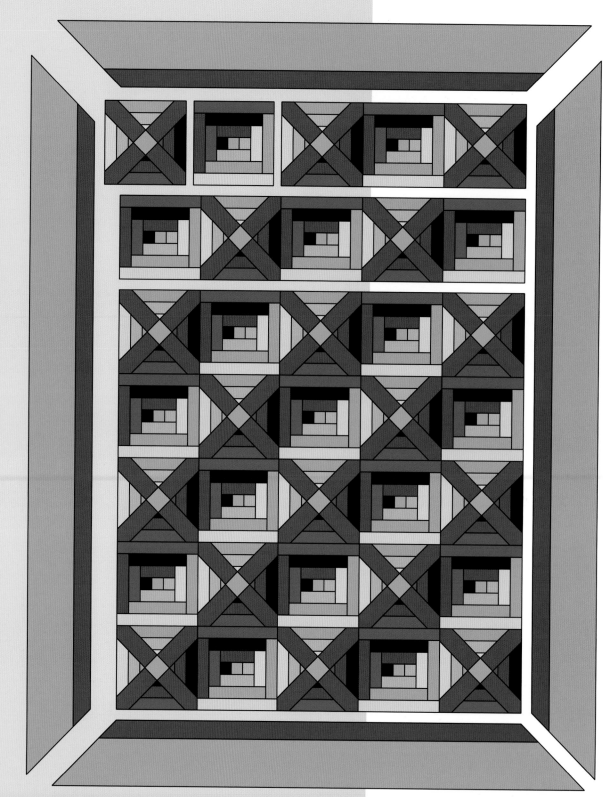

Fig. 22

AROUND THE BLOCK • **TRADITIONAL Two Block Quilts** • Sally Saulmon

Quilt Assembly

1. Make seven rows of five blocks, alternating blocks 1 and 2 in a checkerboard pattern, as shown in the quilt assembly diagram (fig. 22). Make sure the lights and darks are arranged consistently.

2. Sew an inner striped border to an outer large brown print border along their long edges. Repeat for all four borders. Sew the borders to the quilt and miter the corners. Press the seam allowances toward the outside.

Finishing

1. Layer, then quilt as desired.

In the author's quilt, the area between the sashing illusion is hand quilted in an on-point square then echo quilted to fill the space. The X in block 1 and the borders are straight-line quilted in parallel lines.

2. Bind with double-fold, straight-grain binding.

3. Sign and date your quilt.

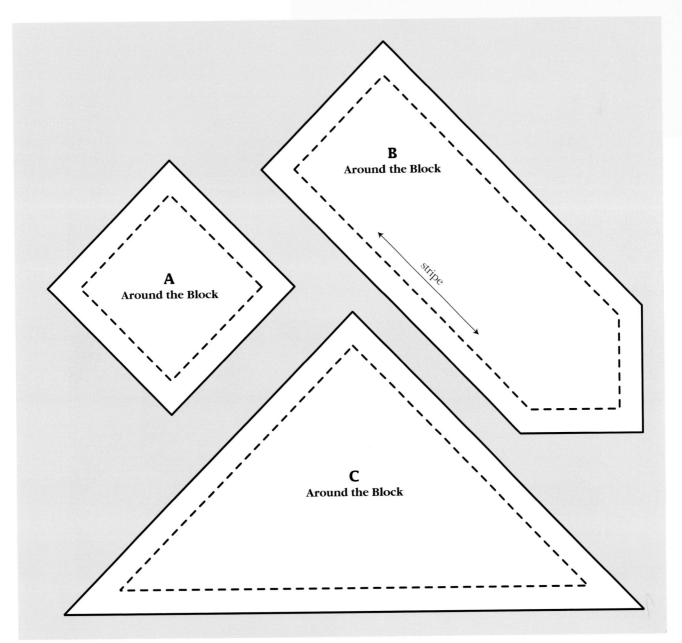

Bountiful Baskets

QUILT SIZE: 49½" x 49½"

BLOCK SIZE: 6"

Fabric Requirements

Yardage is based on 40" wide fabric.

Fabric	Amount
Beige background print	1⅛ yd
Blue stripe	386 running inches by 3½" wide. See Striped Fabric, page 19, for determining yardage.
Assorted blue prints	1 yd total
Assorted purple prints	1⅛ yd total
Backing	3¼ yd (2 panels 28" x 54")
Batting	54" x 54"
Binding	½ yd (6 strips 2½" x 40")

Making Blocks

Patterns are on page 33.

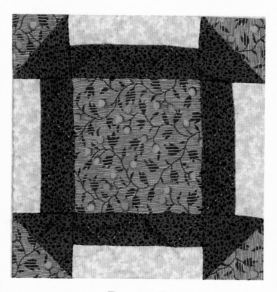

BLOCK 1

BLOCK 2

BOUNTIFUL BASKETS, *by the author. Two different blocks can be placed in a traditional setting, as in this style, which is known as a "strippy." In this quilt, a simple basket block combines beautifully with a Churn Dash variation.*

Fabric	Cutting
Beige background print	72 B rectangles 1¼" x 3½"
Assorted blue prints	18 A squares 3½" x 3½"
	36 C squares 2⅜" x 2⅜" 
Assorted purple prints	72 B rectangles 1¼" x 3½"
	36 C squares 2⅜" x 2⅜"

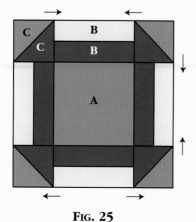

FIG. 23

FIG. 24

FIG. 25

Block 1 Assembly

1. Sew a beige B rectangle to a purple B rectangle (fig. 23). Make four units.

2. Refer to Making Half-Square Units, this page. Use a blue C square and a purple C square to make two half-square triangle units (fig. 24). Make a total of four units.

3. Join an A square, four B units, and four C units to complete a block (fig. 25). Make 18 of block 1.

MAKING HALF-SQUARE UNITS

Use a pencil to mark a diagonal line on the wrong side of a lighter square. Place the square and a darker square right sides together. Sew ¼" on each side of the diagonal line. Cut the units apart on the line and press open. Makes two half-square units.

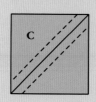

Fabric	Cutting
Beige background print	34 F squares 3⅞" x 3⅞"
Assorted blue prints	17 D squares 3" x 3"
	34 pattern E
	68 pattern I
	17 pattern J
Assorted purple prints	9 D squares 3" x 3"
	68 G squares 2" x 2"
	9 H squares 2¾" x 2¾"
	68 pattern I

Block 2 Assembly

1. Join four blue I triangles and four purple I triangles along their long edges to make four half-square triangle units (fig. 26)

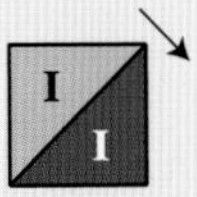

2. Join a blue D triangle and a purple D triangle along their long edges as before (fig. 27).

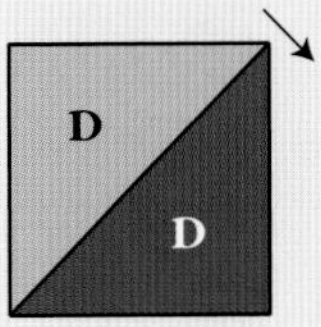

3. Sew purple H triangles to two blue E rectangles, as shown in figure 28. Note that the units are mirror images.

4. Use the Corner-Square Technique, page 20, to add G squares to four F triangles (fig. 29).

5. Join all the pieces to complete the block, as shown in figure 30. Make 17 of block 2.

FIG. 26

FIG. 27

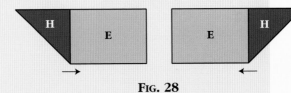

FIG. 28

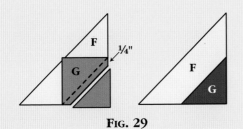

FIG. 29

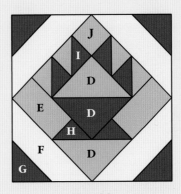

FIG. 30

Border & Sashing Cutting

Border and sashing lengths include 2½" extra for insurance and seam allowances. Strips are cut selvage to selvage and need to be pieced.

Fabric	Cutting
Blue stripe	4 strips 3½" x 44½" for sashing
	4 strips 3½" x 52" for outer border
Beige background print	4 strips 1¼" x 46" for inner border

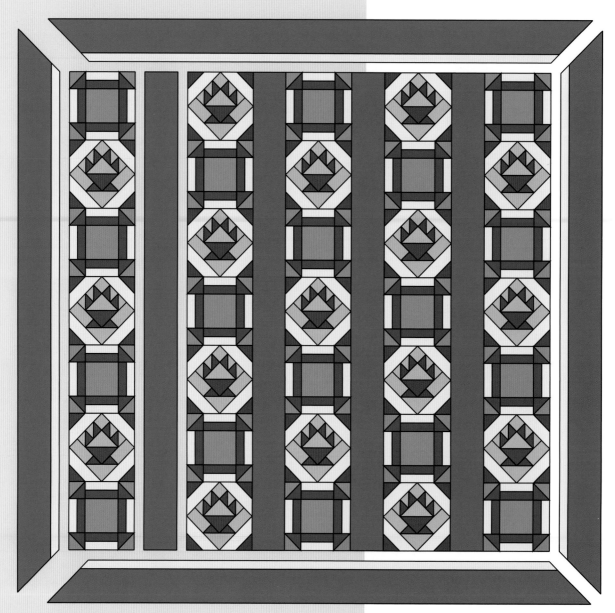

FIG. 31

Quilt Assembly

1. Arrange the blocks in five vertical rows of seven, alternating block 1 and block 2 in a checkerboard pattern. Then add the four blue striped sashing strips in between the rows (fig. 31).

2. Sew an inner border strip to an outer border strip along their long edges. Repeat for all four borders strips. Sew them to the quilt and miter the corners.

Finishing

1. Layer, then quilt as desired.

The author echo quilted block 1 to fill the space. The basket block is quilted in a combination of in-the-ditch and diagonal lines. The sashing and outer border designs follow the pattern printed on the fabric. In-the-ditch quilting completes the inner border.

2. Bind with double-fold, straight-grain binding.

3. Sign and date your quilt.

I Bountiful Baskets

J Bountiful Baskets

E Bountiful Baskets

Centennial Medallion

QUILT SIZE: 40" x 52"

BLOCK SIZE: 6"

Fabric Requirements

Yardage is based on 40" wide fabric.

Fabric	Amount
Pink background print	1 yd
Burgundy stripe	537 running inches by 2⅝" wide. See Striped Fabric, page 19, for determining yardage.
Assorted blue prints	¼ yd total
Assorted green prints	⅝ yd total
Burgundy print	½ yd
Green print	⅜ yd
Backing	2⅝ yd (2 panels 29" x 44")
Batting	44" x 56"
Binding	½ yd (6 strips 2½" x 40")

Making Blocks

Patterns are on page 40.

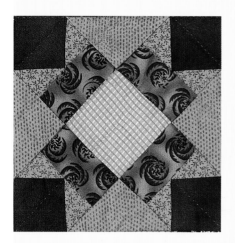

BLOCK 1

BLOCK 2

BLOCK 3

CENTENNIAL MEDALLION, *by the author. This quilt goes a step beyond the two-block theme with the addition of a third block. Notice the appearance of diagonal sashing.*

Fabric	Cutting
Assorted blue prints	19 A squares 2⅝" x 2⅝"
Assorted green prints	76 pattern B
	152 pattern C
Burgundy print	76 D squares 2" x 2"
Pink background print	19 E squares 4¼" x 4¼" ⊠

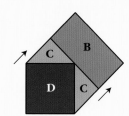

FIG. 32

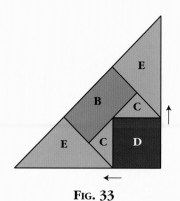

FIG. 33

Block 1 Assembly

1. Sew a B rectangle, two C triangles, and a D square together to make a unit (fig. 32). Make four units.

2. Add two E triangles to the previous unit as shown in figure 33. Make two units.

3. Follow figure 34 to make the center section of the block.

4. Sew all the units together to complete the block (fig. 35). Make 19 of block 1.

FIG. 34

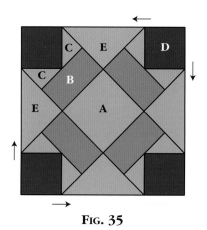

FIG. 35

Block 2 Cutting

Fabric	Cutting
Burgundy print	4 A squares 2⅝" x 2⅝"
Pink background print	4 E squares 4¼" x 4¼" ⊠
Burgundy stripe	16 pattern F

Block 2 Assembly

1. Sew a pink E triangle to each side of a striped F piece (fig. 36). Make two units.

2. Sew a striped F piece to each side of a burgundy A square (fig. 37). Make one unit.

3. Join units to complete the block (fig. 38). Make four of block 2.

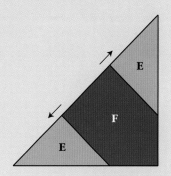

FIG. 36

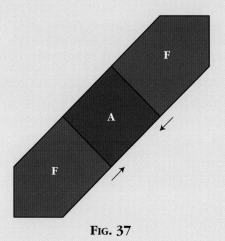

FIG. 37

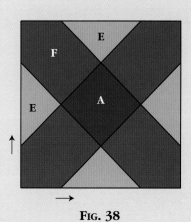

FIG. 38

Block 3 Cutting

Fabric	Cutting
Pink background print	12 G squares 5⅜" x 5⅜" ◹
Burgundy stripe	12 pattern H

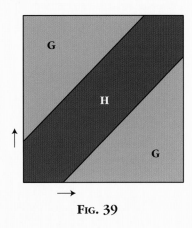

FIG. 39

Block 3 Assembly

Sew a pink G triangle to each side of a striped H piece (fig. 39). Make 12 of block 3.

Border Cutting

Border lengths include 2½" extra for insurance and seam allowances. Border strips are cut selvage to selvage and need to be pieced.

Fabric	Cutting
Burgundy stripe	2 strips 2½" x 36½", top and bottom inner borders
	2 strips 2½" x 48½", side inner borders
	2 strips 2½" x 42½", top and bottom outer borders
	2 strips 2½" x 54½", side outer borders
Green print	2 strips 1½" x 38½", top and bottom middle borders
	2 strips 1½" x 50½", side middle borders

Block and Quilt Assembly

1. Make seven rows of five blocks each, arranging the blocks according to the quilt layout (fig. 40).

2. Sew an inner striped border strip to a middle green border strip, as shown in the quilt layout diagram. Add the outer striped border strip. Repeat for a total of four combined borders.

3. Sew the borders to the quilt and miter the corners. Press the seam allowances toward the striped borders.

Finishing

1. Layer, then quilt as desired.

In the author's quilt, hand quilting radiates out from the center of the medallion. In the striped fabric, the quilting design follows the paisleys. In-the-ditch quilting, where needed, completes the design.

2. Bind with double-fold, straight-grain binding.

3. Sign and date your quilt.

FIG. 40

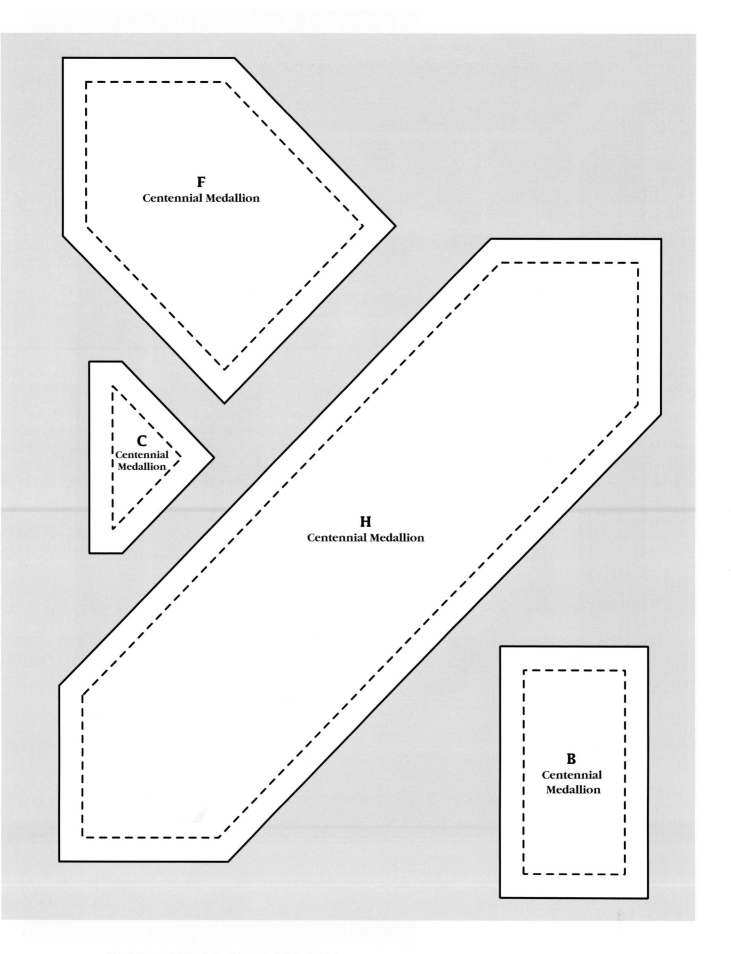

F
Centennial Medallion

C
Centennial
Medallion

H
Centennial Medallion

B
Centennial
Medallion

Country Road

QUILT SIZE: 47½" x 47½"
BLOCK SIZE: 7½"

Fabric Requirements

Yardage is based on 40" wide fabric.

Fabric	Amount
Light beige background print	⅞ yd
Tan background print	1¼ yd
Assorted rust prints	¾ yd total
Assorted green prints	1 yd total
Green print	⅞ yd
Backing	3⅛ yd (2 panels 27" x 52")
Batting	52" x 52"
Binding	½ yd (6 strips 2½" x 40")

Making Blocks

Patterns are on page 46.

BLOCK 1

BLOCK 2

COUNTRY ROAD, *by the author. Combining a traditional pieced block with an appliquéd block brought back memories of many country roads.*

Block 1 Cutting

Fabric	Cutting
Light beige background print	26 A squares 3⅜" x 3⅜" ◻
Tan background print	26 A squares 3⅜" x 3⅜" ◻
Assorted rust prints	130 B squares 1¾" x 1¾"
Assorted green prints	130 B squares 1¾" x 1¾"

Block 1 Assembly

1. Using light beige print A squares and tan print A squares, make four half-square units (fig. 41).

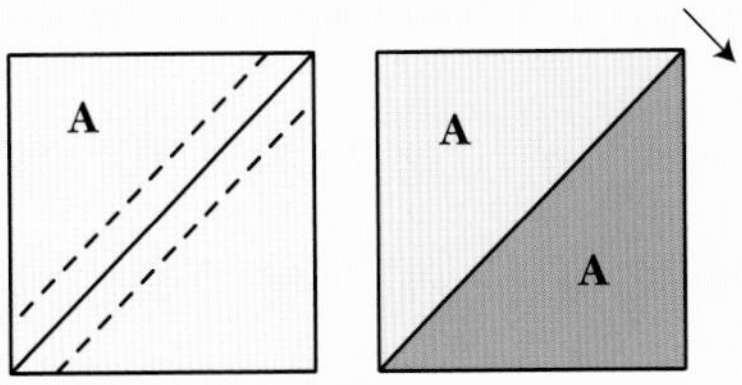

2. Referring to figure 42, make five four-patch units from the rust and green B squares.

3. Alternating the units, sew them together as shown in figure 43 to complete the block. Make 13 of block 1.

FIG. 41

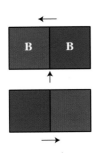

FIG. 42

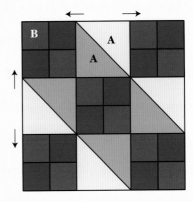

FIG. 43

Block 2 Cutting

Fabric	Cutting
Light beige background print	48 C squares 3" x 3"
Tan background print	60 C squares 3" x 3"
Assorted rust prints (includes border flowers)	32 pattern D 12 pattern E 32 pattern F
Assorted green prints (includes border leaves)	12 pattern G 32 pattern Gr 290 running inches by 1¼" wide, bias strips for stems

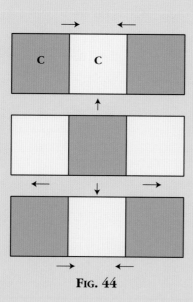

FIG. 44

Block 2 assembly

1. Alternating five tan C squares and four beige C squares, sew them together as shown in figure 44 to complete the background block for the appliqué.

2. Using your favorite appliqué method, prepare and sew appliqué pieces to the background block (fig. 45). Make 12 of block 2.

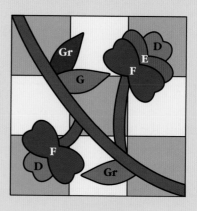

FIG. 45

Border Cutting

Border lengths include 2½" extra for insurance and seam allowances. Border strips are cut selvage to selvage and need to be pieced.

Fabric	Cutting
Tan background print	4 strips 1¾" x 42½", inner borders
Green print	4 strips 4¼" x 50", outer borders

Quilt Assembly

1. Make five rows of five blocks each, alternating block 1 and block 2 in a checkerboard pattern as shown in the quilt layout (fig. 46).

2. Sew an inner tan border strip to a green border strip along their long edges. Repeat for a total of four borders.

3. Appliqué the flowers, leaves, and stems to each border as shown in the quilt layout diagram. Sew the borders to the quilt and miter the corners.

Finishing

1. Layer, then quilt as desired.

The entire quilt in the photo on page 41 is hand quilted in parallel, diagonal lines spaced 1" apart. All of the appliqué pieces are outline quilted in the ditch.

2. Bind with double-fold, straight-grain binding.

3. Sign and date your quilt.

FIG. 46

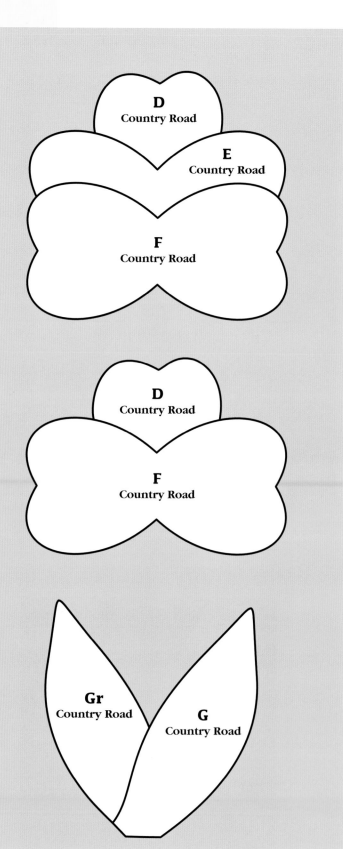

D
Country Road

E
Country Road

F
Country Road

D
Country Road

F
Country Road

Gr
Country Road

G
Country Road

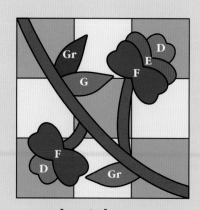

appliqué placement

Garden Maze

QUILT SIZE: 47½" x 47½"

BLOCK SIZE: 7"

Fabric Requirements

Yardage is based on 40" wide fabric.

Fabric	Amount
Light green print	½ yd
Medium green large print	1⅛ yd. Buy extra yardage if C or E patches are fussy cut.
Medium green small print	⅞ yd
Dark green print	1⅛ yd
Red print	⅝ yd
Backing	3⅛ yd (2 panels 27" x 52")
Batting	52" x 52"
Binding	½ yd (6 strips 2½" x 40")

Making Blocks

BLOCK 1

BLOCK 2

GARDEN MAZE

GARDEN MAZE, *by the author, machine quilted by Judy Case of Florence, Colorado. Two blocks are combined and then set on point to create an interlocking secondary pattern.*

Block 1 Cutting

Fabric	Cutting
Light green print	16 A squares 3½" x 3½"
Medium green small print	64 B rectangles 2½" x 3½"
Medium green large print	32 C squares 2⅞" x 2⅞"
Dark green print	32 C squares 2⅞" x 2⅞"
	192 D squares 1½" x 1½"

Block 1 Assembly

1. Using the corner-square technique, sew four dark green D squares to a light green A square (fig. 47). Make one unit.

2. Use the corner-square method to sew two dark green D squares to a medium green B rectangle (fig. 48). Make four units.

3. Use medium green C squares and dark green C squares to make four half-square units (fig. 49).

4. Sew the units into rows then sew the rows together to complete the block (fig. 50). Make 16 of block 1.

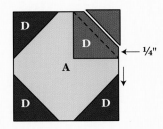

FIG. 47

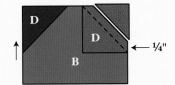

FIG. 48

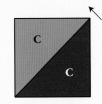

FIG. 49

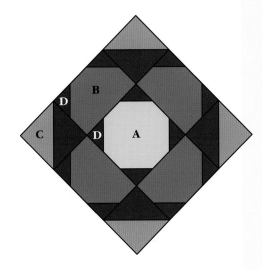

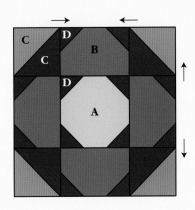

FIG. 50

Fabric	Cutting
Medium green small print	9 A squares 3½" x 3½"
	36 F rectangles 1½" x 2½"
Medium green large print	36 E squares 2½" x 2½"
Dark green print	36 D squares 1½" x 1½" ◩
	72 F rectangles 1½" x 2½"

Block 2 Assembly

1. Using the corner-square technique, sew four dark green D squares to a medium green A square (fig. 51). Make one unit.

2. Sew a dark green F rectangle to each side of a medium green F rectangle (fig. 52). Make four units.

3. Join the pieces as shown in figure 53 to complete the block. Make nine of block 2.

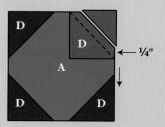

FIG. 51

FIG. 52

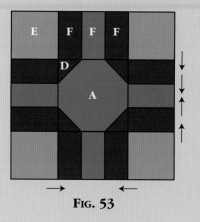

FIG. 53

Setting Triangle Cutting

Fabric	Cutting
Red print	2 squares 5⅞" x 5⅞" ◹ = 4 corner triangles
	3 squares 11⅛" x 11⅛" ⊠ = 12 side triangles

Border Cutting

Border lengths include 2½" extra for insurance and seam allowances. Border strips are cut selvage to selvage and need to be pieced.

Fabric	Cutting
Light green print	2 strips 1½" x 42½", top and bottom inner borders
	2 strips 1½" x 44½", side inner borders
Medium green large print	2 strips 3½" x 44½", top and bottom outer borders
	2 strips 3½" x 50½", side outer borders

Quilt Assembly

1. Setting the blocks on point, alternate block 1 and block 2 in a checkerboard pattern, adding the red setting triangles as shown in the quilt layout (fig. 54, page 52).

2. Sew the light green top and bottom inner borders on the quilt. Sew the remaining light green border strips to the sides of the quilt.

3. In the same way, add the outer medium green borders.

Finishing

1. Layer, then quilt as desired.
  In the author's quilt, the body is machine quilted in an overall, swirling design, and vine designs accent the borders.

2. Bind with double-fold, straight-grain binding.

3. Sign and date your quilt.

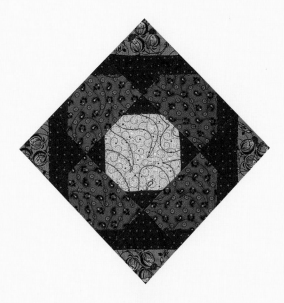

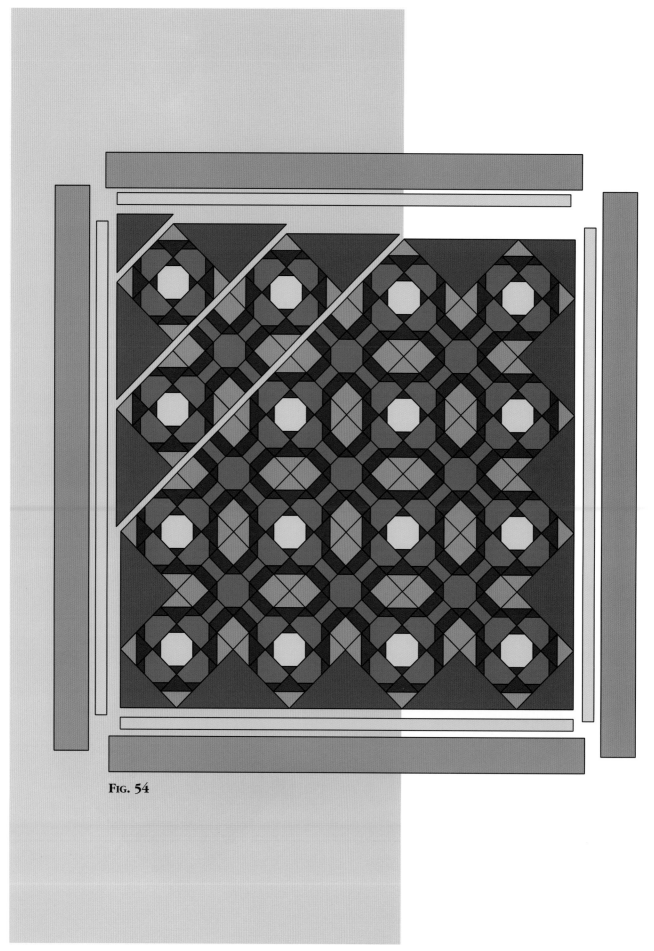

FIG. 54

• **TRADITIONAL Two Block Quilts** • Sally Saulmon

Hoopla

QUILT SIZE: 54" x 54"
BLOCK SIZE: 6"

Fabric Requirements

Yardage is based on 40" wide fabric.

Fabric	Amount
Blue and red print	1 yd
Beige background print	½ yd
Assorted red prints	1¼ yd total
Assorted blue prints	¾ yd total
Red and white stripe	334 running inches by 3½" wide. See Striped Fabric, page 19, for determining yardage.
Backing	3½ yd (2 panels 30" x 58")
Batting	58" x 58"
Binding	½ yd (6 strips 2½" x 40")

Making Blocks

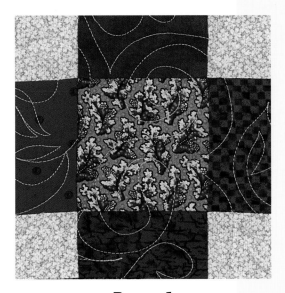

BLOCK 1

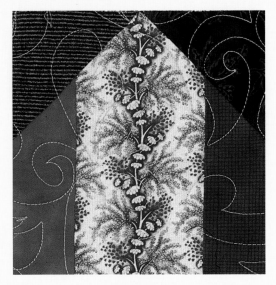

BLOCK 2

HOOPLA

HOOPLA, *by the author, machine quilted by Judy Case of Florence, Colorado. Two simple blocks are combined to provide movement.*

Fabric	Cutting
Blue and red print	29 A squares 3½" x 3½"
Assorted red prints	116 B rectangles 2" x 3½"
Beige background print	116 C squares 2" x 2"

Block 1 Assembly

1. Sew a beige C square on each side of a red B rectangle (fig. 55). Make two units.

2. Sew a red B rectangle to each side of a blue and red A square (fig. 56). Make one unit.

3. Join the units to complete the block (fig. 57). Make 29 of block 1.

FIG. 55

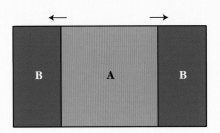

FIG. 56

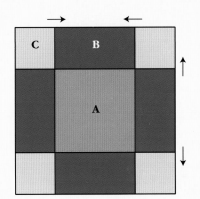

FIG. 57

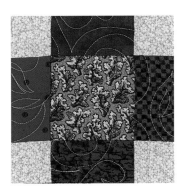

Block 2 Cutting

Fabric	Cutting
Red and white stripe	24 D rectangles 3½" x 6½"
Assorted red prints	48 E rectangles 2" x 6½"
Assorted blue prints	48 F squares 3½" x 3½"

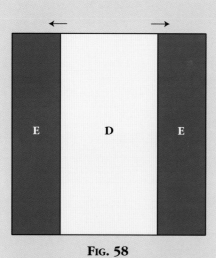

FIG. 58

Block 2 Assembly

1. Sew a red E rectangle to each side of a striped D rectangle (fig. 58). Make one unit.

2. Using the corner-square technique, add F squares to the D/E unit, as shown in figure 59. Make 24 of block 2.

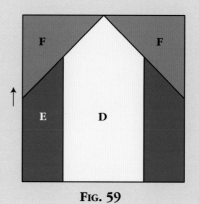

FIG. 59

Border Cutting

Border lengths include 2½" extra for insurance and seam allowances. Border strips are cut selvage to selvage and need to be pieced.

Fabric	Cutting
Blue and red print	8 strips 2" x 44½", inner and outer borders
Red and white stripe	4 strips 3½" x 44½", middle borders

Quilt Assembly

1. Arrange seven rows of seven blocks each, alternating block 1 and block 2 in a checkerboard pattern, as shown in the quilt layout (fig. 60, page 57). Take care that directional block 2 is rotated correctly to reveal the pattern.

2. Sew a blue/red border strip to each side of a striped border strip. Repeat to make a total of four border units.

3. Sew a border unit to each side of the quilt.

4. Sew a block 1 to each short side of the remaining two border units.

5. Sew these borders to the top and bottom of the quilt.

Finishing

1. Layer, then quilt as desired.

   The quilt in the photo on page 53 is machine quilted in an overall, swirling design.

2. Bind with double-fold, straight-grain binding.

3. Sign and date your quilt.

Fig. 60

Moonglow

QUILT SIZE: 54" x 54"
BLOCK SIZE: 4½"

Fabric Requirements

Yardage is based on 40" wide fabric.

Fabric	Amount
Dark blue print	⅝ yd
Medium blue print	½ yd
Light blue print	½ yd
Pale blue print	¼ yd
Dark purple print	⅝ yd
Medium purple print	⅝ yd
Light purple print	⅜ yd
Lilac print	¼ yd
Black print	1⅜ yd
Purple-blue print	1 yd
Backing	3½ yd (2 panels 30" x 58")
Batting	58" x 58"
Binding	½ yd (6 strips 2½" x 40")

Making Blocks

Patterns are on page 64.

BLOCK 1

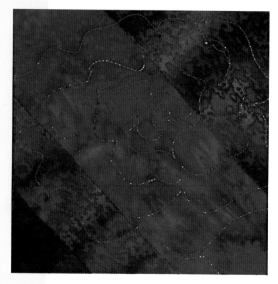

BLOCK 2

• **TRADITIONAL Two Block Quilts** • Sally Saulmon

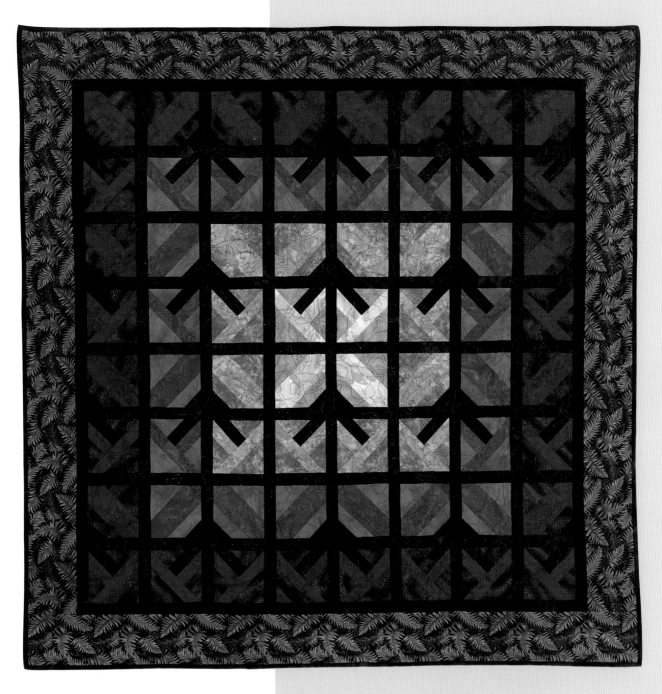

MOONGLOW, *by the author, machine quilted by Judy Case of Florence, Colorado. The use of a gradation of fabrics, plus the use of sashing between the two blocks, produces interesting secondary patterns.*

Fabric	Cutting
Dark blue print	14 pattern A 7 pattern B 7 pattern Br
Medium blue print	10 pattern A 5 pattern B 5 pattern Br
Light blue print	6 pattern A 3 pattern B 3 pattern Br
Pale blue print	2 pattern A 1 pattern B 1 pattern Br
Dark purple print	7 C squares 4¼" x 4¼" ⊠ 7 D squares 3⅞" x 3⅞" ◻
Medium purple print	5 C squares 4¼" x 4¼" ⊠ 5 D squares 3⅞" x 3⅞" ◻
Light purple print	3 C squares 4¼" x 4¼" ⊠ 3 D squares 3⅞" x 3⅞" ◻
Lilac print	1 C square 4¼" x 4¼" ⊠ 1 D square 3⅞" x 3⅞" ◻
Black print	16 pattern B 16 pattern Br

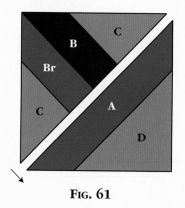

FIG. 61

Block 1 Assembly

Follow the block assembly diagram (fig. 61) to make 16 of block 1 in the following color combinations:

7 dark blue (A & Br) and dark purple (C & D), with black in position B

5 medium blue (A & Br) and medium purple (C & D), with black in position B

3 light blue (A & Br) and light purple (C & D), with black in position B

1 pale blue (A & Br) and lilac (C & D), with black in position B

Reverse Block 1 Assembly

Follow the block assembly diagram (fig. 62) to make 16 of reverse block 1 in the following color combinations:

7 dark blue (A & B) and dark purple (C & D), with black in position Br

5 medium blue (A & B) and medium purple (C & D), with black in position Br

3 light blue (A & B) and light purple (C & D), with black in position Br

1 pale blue (A & B) and lilac (C & D), with black in position Br

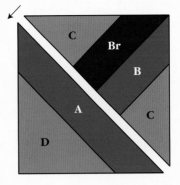

FIG. 62

Block 2 Cutting

Fabric	Cutting
Dark blue print	14 pattern E
Medium blue print	10 pattern E
Light blue print	6 pattern E
Pale blue print	2 pattern E
Dark purple print	14 pattern F 7 D squares 3⅞" x 3⅞" ◻
Medium purple print	10 pattern F 5 D squares 3⅞" x 3⅞" ◻
Light purple print	6 pattern F 3 D squares 3⅞" x 3⅞" ◻
Lilac print	2 pattern F 1 D square 3⅞" x 3⅞" ◻
Black print	16 G squares 2⅜" x 2⅜" ◻

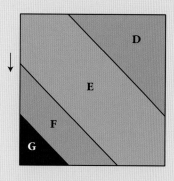

Fig. 63

Block 2 Assembly

Follow the block assembly diagram (fig. 63) to make 32 of block 2 in the following color combinations:

14 dark blue (E) and dark purple (D & F), with black in position G

10 medium blue (E) and medium purple (D & F), with black in position G.

6 light blue (E) and light purple (D & F), with black in position G.

2 pale blue (E) and lilac (D & F), with black in position G.

Sashing and Border Cutting

Sashing and border lengths include 2½" extra for insurance and seam allowances. Strips are cut selvage to selvage and need to be pieced.

Fabric	Cutting
Black print	56 rectangles 1½" x 5", sashing
	7 strips 1½" x 45½", sashing
	2 strips 1½" x 45½", inner borders
	2 strips 1½" x 47½", inner borders
Blue-purple print	2 strips 5" x 47½", outer borders
	2 strips 5" x 56½", outer borders

Quilt Assembly

1. Refer to the quilt photo and figure 64, page 63 for color placement. Make eight rows of eight blocks each, arranging the blocks from light in the middle to dark on the edge.

2. Sew the vertical rows together with short sashing strips between the blocks.

3. Sew the rows together with the long sashing strips between them.

4. Sew the two black side inner borders to the quilt then add the black top and bottom inner borders.

5. In the same way, add the blue-purple outer borders.

Finishing

1. Layer, then quilt as desired.

In the author's quilt, leaf and fern machine quilting covers the body of the quilt. A similar design, accented with in-the-ditch quilting, was used in the borders.

2. Bind with double-fold, straight-grain binding.

3. Sign and date your quilt.

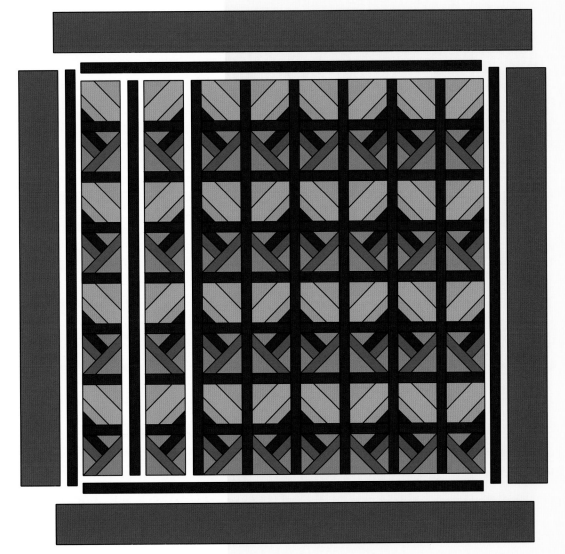

FIG. 64

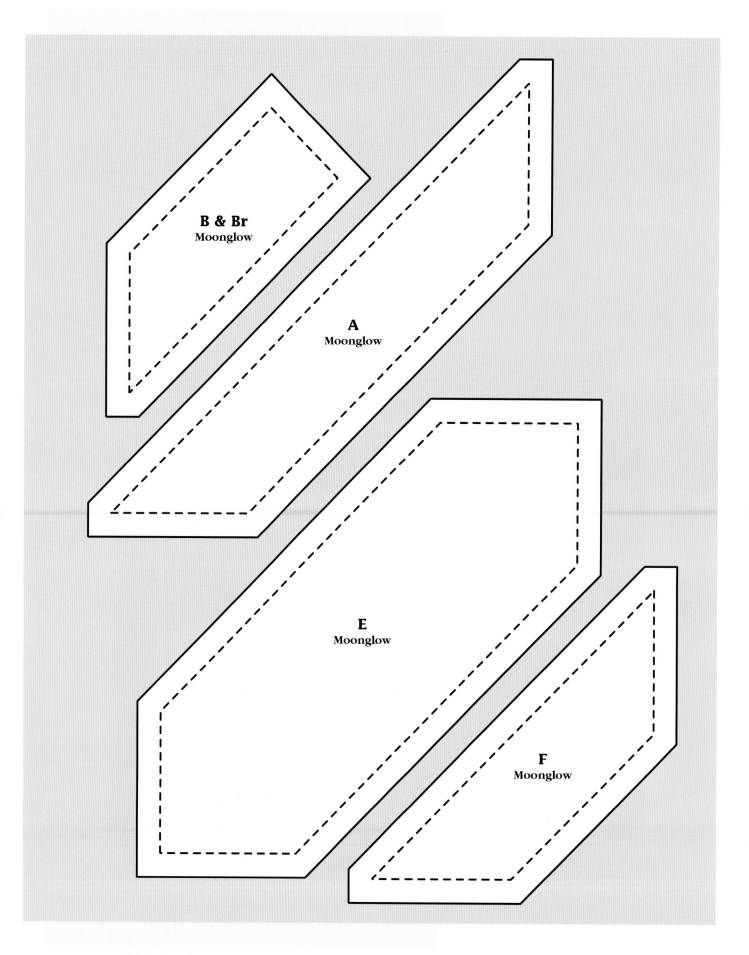

B & Br
Moonglow

A
Moonglow

E
Moonglow

F
Moonglow

• TRADITIONAL Two Block Quilts • Sally Saulmon

Mother's Kitchen

QUILT SIZE: 41" x 41"
BLOCK SIZE: 5"

Fabric Requirements

Yardage is based on 40" wide fabric.

Fabric	Amount
White background print	1¼ yd
Red print	¾ yd
Pink check	¾ yd
Blue check	¾ yd
Blue print	½ yd
Green print	¼ yd
Backing	2⅝ yd (2 panels 23" x 45")
Batting	45" x 45"
Binding	½ yd (5 strips 2½" x 40")

Making Blocks

Patterns are on page 70.

BLOCK 1

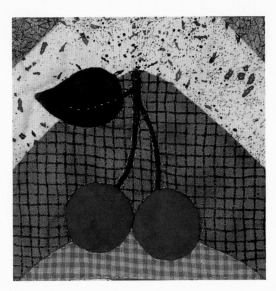

BLOCK 2

MOTHER'S KITCHEN

MOTHER'S KITCHEN, *by the author. Combining a checkerboard block with appliquéd cherry blocks and using fabrics reminiscent of the 1950s brings back memories of the kitchens of our mothers and grandmothers.*

Fabric	Cutting
White background print	12 strips 1½" x 40"
Red print	9 strips 1½" x 40"
Pink check	4 strips 1½" x 40"

Block 1 Assembly

1. Sew two A strip-sets, each combining two pink strips, two white strips, and one red strip. From the strip-sets, cut a total of 50 units 1½" wide (fig. 65).

2. Sew two B strip-sets, each combining three white strips and two red strips. From the strip-sets, cut a total of 50 units 1½" wide (fig. 66).

3. Sew one C strip-set, combining three red strips and two white strips. Cut the strip-set into 25 units 1½" wide (fig. 67).

4. As shown in figure 68, sew two A units, two B units, and 1 C unit together to complete the block. Make 25 of block 1.

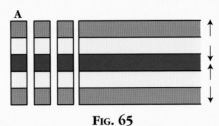

FIG. 65

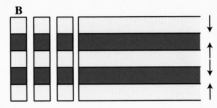

FIG. 66

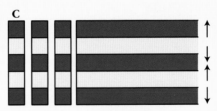

FIG. 67

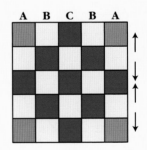

FIG. 68

Fabric	Cutting
Blue print	48 A squares 1½" x 1½"
White background print	24 B rectangles 4½" x 5½"
Pink check	24 C rectangles 1½" x 5½"
Blue check	24 pattern D
Red print	48 pattern E
Green print	24 pattern F

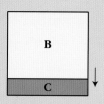

FIG. 69

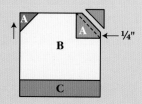

FIG. 70

Block 2 Assembly

1. Sew a white background B rectangle to a pink checked C rectangle (fig. 69).

2. Use the corner-square method to add the A squares to the B/C unit (fig. 70).

3. Using your favorite method, prepare and sew the appliqué pieces to the B/C unit (fig. 71). The cherry stems are satin-stitched with brown thread. Make 24 of block 2.

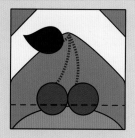

FIG. 71

Quilt assembly

1. Join seven rows of seven blocks each, alternating block 1 and block 2 in a checkerboard pattern (fig. 72, page 69). Take care that the directional appliqué block is rotated correctly to reveal the pattern.

Border Cutting

Border lengths include 2½" extra for insurance and seam allowances. Border strips are cut selvage to selvage.

Fabric	Cutting
Pink check	4 strips 1½" x 37½", inner borders
Red print	12 squares 1½" x 1½", corner blocks
White background print	8 squares 1½" x 1½", corner blocks
Blue print	4 strips 2½" x 39½", outer borders

2. Sew pink checked border strips to two opposite sides of the quilt. Add red corner squares to the ends of the remaining pink checked borders then sew them to the quilt.

3. For each outer corner block, sew two white and two red 1½" squares in checkerboard fashion. Add the outer borders in the same manner as the pink checked inner border.

Finishing

1. Layer, then quilt as desired.

In the author's quilt, the checkerboard block is hand quilted in a crosshatching pattern, and the cherry block is accented with in-the-ditch and outline quilting. A meandering leaf pattern covers the borders.

2. Bind with double-fold, straight-grain binding.

3. Sign and date your quilt.

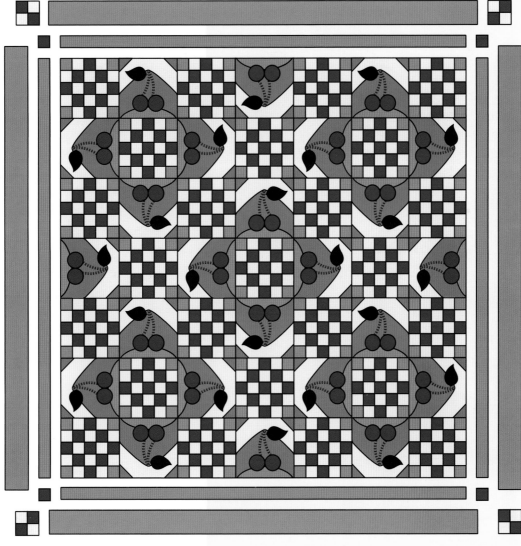

Fig. 72

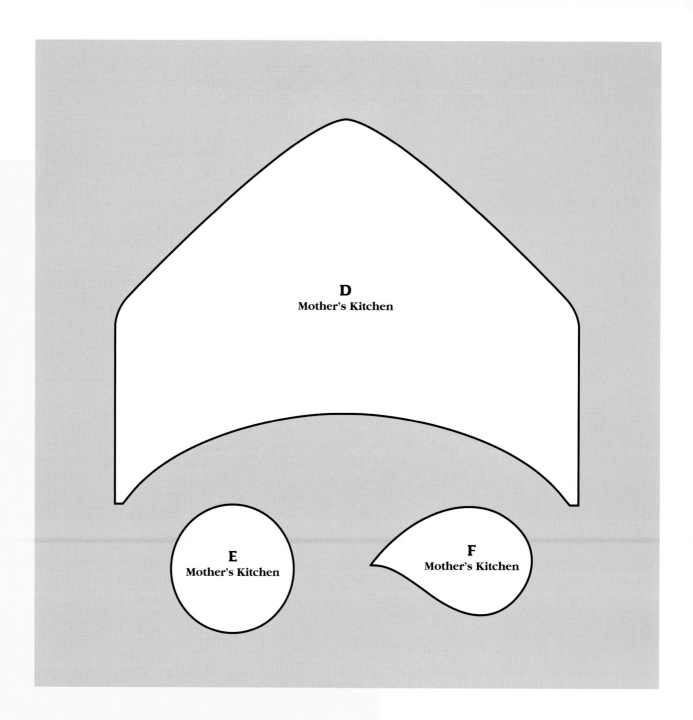

D
Mother's Kitchen

E
Mother's Kitchen

F
Mother's Kitchen

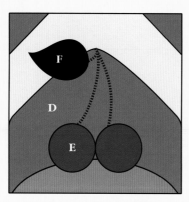

appliqué placement

Persian Puzzle

QUILT SIZE: 38" x 38"

BLOCK SIZE: 6" x 10"

Fabric Requirements

Yardage is based on 40" wide fabric.

Fabric	Amount
Beige background print	⅝ yd
Red print	½ yd
Taupe print	½ yd
Red paisley print	1 yd; buy extra yardage if A or F patches are fussy cut.
Taupe stripe	240 running inches by 2" wide. See Striped Fabric, page 19, for determining yardage.
Backing	1¼ yd (1 panel 42" x 42") or 2½ yd (2 panels 22" x 42")
Batting	42" x 42"
Binding	½ yd (5 strips 2½" x 40")

Making Blocks

Patterns are on page 76.

BLOCK 1

BLOCK 2

PERSIAN PUZZLE, *by the author. Blocks do not have to be square! In this quilt, two rectangular blocks have been combined to produce many secondary patterns.*

Fabric	Cutting
Red paisley print	8 A squares 4½" x 4½"
Beige background print	16 B rectangles 1½" x 4½"
	8 E squares 3¼" x 3¼" ☒
Red print	16 C rectangles 1½" x 6½"
	4 E squares 3¼" x 3¼" ☒
Taupe print	16 D squares 2⅞" x 2⅞" ◺
	4 E squares 3¼" x 3¼" ☒
Taupe stripe	32 pattern D

Block 1 Assembly

1. Sew a beige B rectangle to each side of a red paisley A square (fig. 73). Make one unit.

2. Sew a taupe D triangle to a stripe D triangle as shown in figure 74. Make four units.

3. Join four E triangles in the color order shown in figure 75. Make two units.

4. Join all the units and two C rectangles to complete the block (fig. 76). Make eight of block 1.

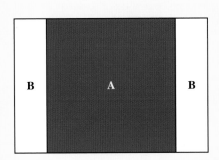

FIG. 73

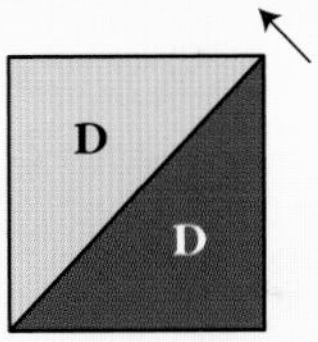

FIG. 74

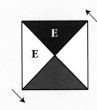

FIG. 75

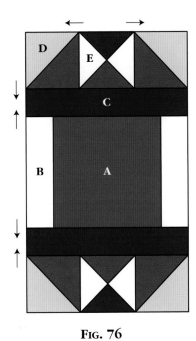

FIG. 76

Fabric	Cutting
Taupe stripe	28 pattern D
Red paisley print	14 F squares 3⅞" x 3⅞" 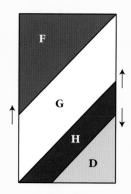
Beige background print	14 pattern G
	14 pattern G reversed
Red print	28 pattern H

FIG. 77

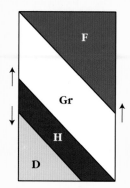

FIG. 78

Block 2 Assembly

1. Join an F, G, H, and D patch as shown in figure 77 to make a quarter of the block. Make 14 units.

2. Join an F, Gr, H, and D patch to make another quarter of the block (fig. 78). Note that this unit is the mirror image of the first unit. Make 14 units.

3. Sew together four units to complete a block (fig. 79). Make seven of block 2.

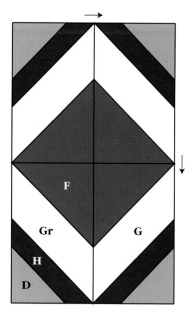

FIG. 79

Border Cutting

Border lengths include 2½" extra for insurance and seam allowances. Border strips are cut selvage to selvage and may need to be pieced.

Fabric	Cutting
Taupe print	4 strips 1½" x 34½", inner borders
Red paisley print	4 strips 3½" x 40½", outer borders

Quilt Assembly

1. Join three rows of five blocks each, alternating block 1 and block 2 in a checkerboard pattern as shown figure 80.

2. Sew an inner taupe border to a red paisley border along their long edges. Repeat for a total of four borders.

3. Sew the borders to the quilt and miter the corners.

Finishing

1. Layer, then quilt as desired.

The author hand quilted the blocks in a combination of echo and in-the-ditch design. The medallions in each block and the paisley border were quilted following the pattern design in the fabric.

2. Bind with double-fold, straight-grain binding.

3. Sign and date your quilt.

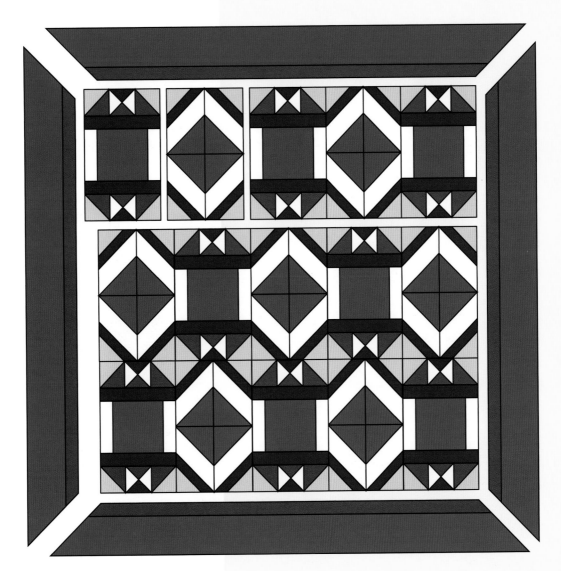

FIG. 80

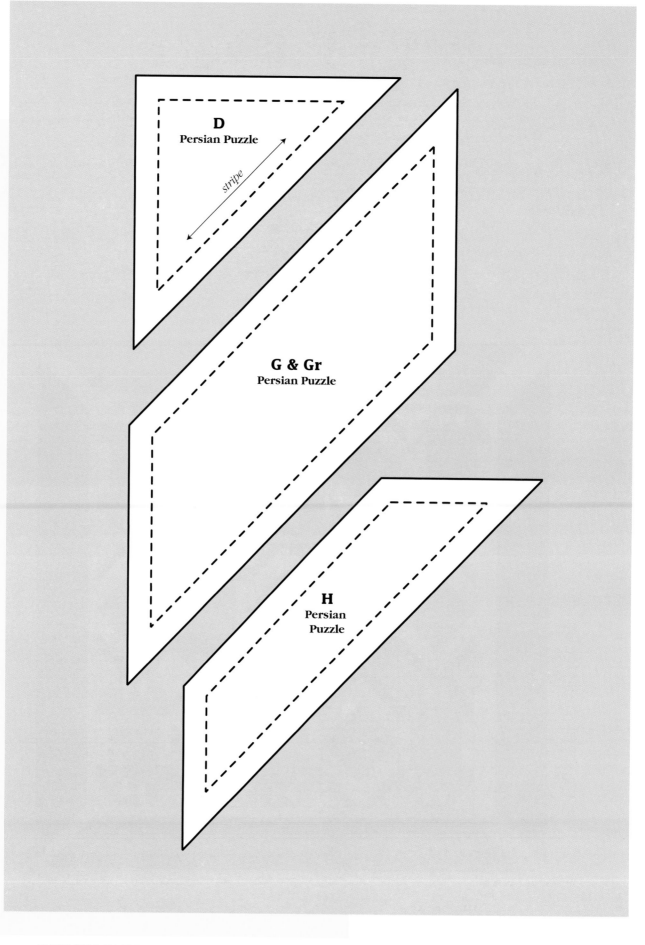

D
Persian Puzzle

stripe

G & Gr
Persian Puzzle

H
Persian
Puzzle

• **TRADITIONAL Two Block Quilts** • Sally Saulmon

Retro Rockets

QUILT SIZE: 46½" x 46½"

BLOCK SIZE: 7½"

Fabric Requirements

Yardage is based on 40" wide fabric.

Fabric	Amount
Lilac solid	⅝ yd
Purple solid	⅝ yd
Black solid	1½ yd
Assorted 1930s' reproduction prints	1 yd total
Backing	3 yd (2 panels 26" x 51")
Batting	51" x 51"
Binding	½ yd (6 strips 2½" x 40")

Making Blocks

Patterns are on page 82.

BLOCK 1

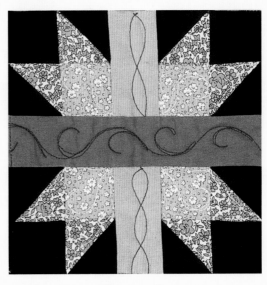

BLOCK 2

RETRO ROCKETS, *by the author, machine quilted by Judy Case of Florence, Colorado. Combining a block that has a 60-degree angle triangle with a star block produces the illusion of circles from straight lines. These two blocks also produce the illusion of a woven sashing.*

Fabric	Cutting
Lilac solid	13 A rectangles 2" x 8"
Purple solid	26 B rectangles 2" x 3½"
Assorted 1930s' reproduction prints	26 C squares 2⅜" x 2⅜" ◻
	52 pattern D
Black solid	52 pattern E
	52 pattern E reversed

Block 1 Assembly

1. Referring to figure 81, sew a black E and a black E reversed to each side of a print D. Add a reproduction C triangle. Make four units.

2. Join the four units with two B rectangles and an A rectangle, as shown in figure 82, to complete the block. Make 13 of block 1.

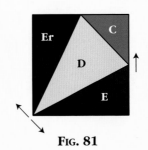

FIG. 81

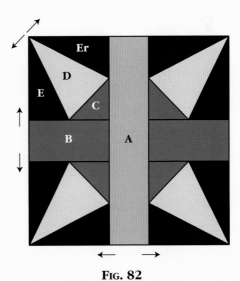

FIG. 82

Fabric	Cutting
Purple solid	12 A rectangles 2" x 8"
Lilac solid	24 B rectangles 2" x 3½"
Black solid	48 F squares 2" x 2"
	48 G squares 2⅜" x 2⅜" ◻
Assorted 1930s' reproduction prints	48 F squares 2" x 2"
	48 G squares 2⅜" x 2⅜" ◻

FIG. 83

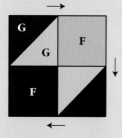

FIG. 84

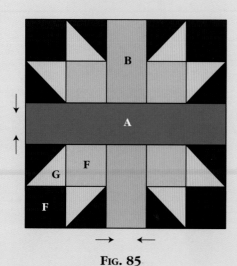

FIG. 85

Block 2 Assembly

1. Using reproduction G squares and black G squares, make eight half-square units (fig. 83).

2. Add a black F square and a reproduction F square to two of the half-square units, as shown in figure 84. Make four F/G units.

3. Join the four F/G units with two B rectangles and an A rectangle, as shown in figure 85, to complete the block. Make 12 of block 2.

Border Cutting

Border lengths include 2½" extra for insurance and seam allowances. Border strips are cut selvage to selvage and need to be pieced.

Fabric	Cutting
Lilac solid	2 strips 2" x 43", inner side borders
Purple solid	2 strips 2" x 43", top and bottom inner borders
Black solid	4 strips 3½" x 49", outer borders

Quilt Assembly

1. Make five rows of five blocks each, alternating block 1 and block 2 in a checkerboard pattern, as shown in the quilt layout (fig. 86).

2. Sew an inner lilac border to two of the black outer borders along their long edges, and an inner purple border to the remaining two black borders. Sew the combined borders to quilt and miter the corners.

Finishing

1. Layer, then quilt as desired.

The blocks in the author's quilt are outline machine quilted with accents of a swirling motif. Cables and a swirling design cover the sashing, and an overall design of hearts was used in the border.

2. Bind with double-fold, straight-grain binding.

3. Sign and date your quilt.

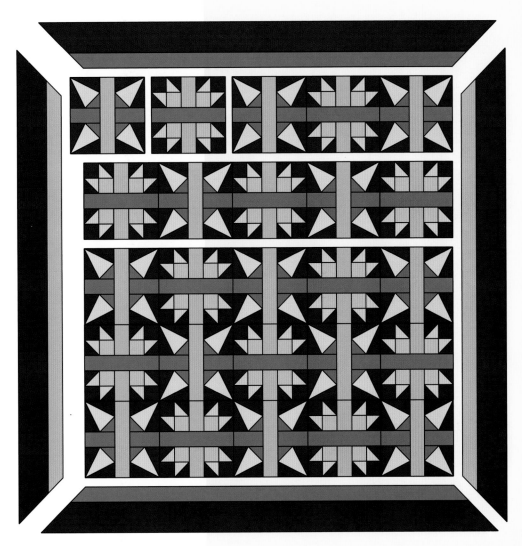

FIG. 86

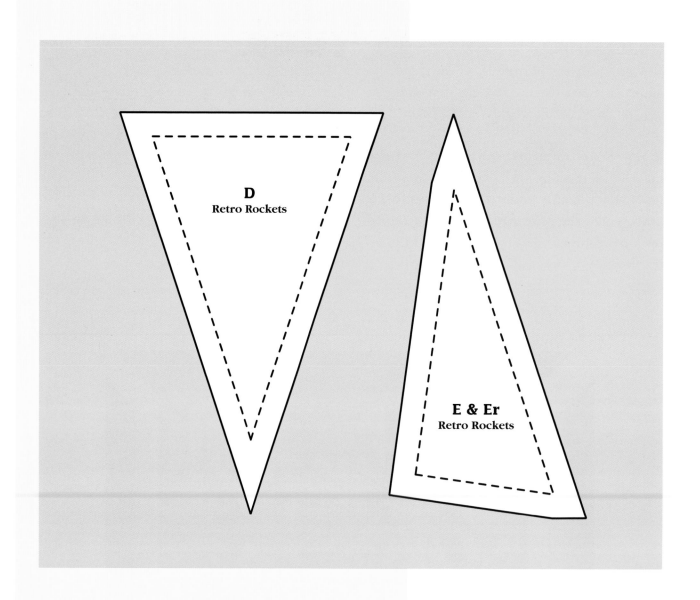

D
Retro Rockets

E & Er
Retro Rockets

Starstruck

Fabric Requirements

Yardage is based on 40" wide fabric.

Fabric	Amount
Black	1⅛ yd
Green stripe	630 running inches by 2" wide. See Striped Fabric, page 19, for determining yardage.
Assorted red prints	1¼ yd total
Assorted light and dark green prints	2⅜ yd total
Assorted yellow prints	1⅜ yd total
Yellow print	⅝ yd
Red print	¾ yd
Backing	4 yd (2 panels 35" x 68")
Batting	68" x 68"
Binding	⅝ yd (7 strips 2½" x 40")

Making Blocks

Patterns are on page 86.

BLOCK 1

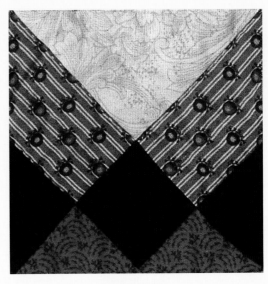

BLOCK 2

STARSTRUCK

STARSTRUCK, *by the author. By using color and value and rotating the directional block, interlocking patterns are revealed.*

Fabric	Cutting
Assorted red prints	24 A squares 2½" x 2½"
	192 B squares 1½" x 1½"
Assorted dark green prints	61 A squares 2½" x 2½"
	488 B squares 1½" x 1½"
Assorted light green prints	240 C rectangles 1½" x 2½"
	240 D squares 1½" x 1½"
Assorted yellow prints	100 C rectangles 1½" x 2½"
	100 D squares 1½" x 1½"

Block 1 Assembly

1. Use the corner-square technique to make the B/C units (fig. 87). Make four units.

2. Add a D square to each side of a B/C unit (fig. 88). Make two units.

3. Add a B/C unit to two opposite sides of an A square (fig. 89).

4. Join the units to complete a block (fig. 90).

5. Make block 1 in the following color combinations and quantities:

25 blocks with green stars on a yellow background

24 with red stars on a green background

36 with green stars on a lighter green background

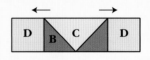

FIG. 87

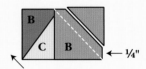

FIG. 88

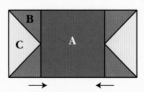

FIG. 89

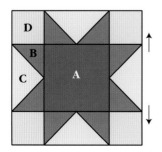
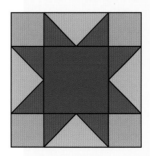
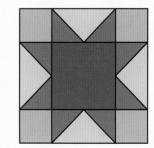

FIG. 90

Fabric	Cutting
Black print	84 pattern F
	42 E squares 3¼" x 3¼" ⊠
Green stripe	84 pattern G
	84 pattern G reversed
Assorted red prints	42 E squares 3¼" x 3¼" ⊠
Assorted yellow prints	21 H squares 5¼" x 5¼" ⊠

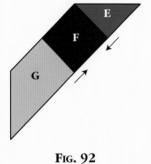

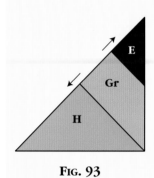

Fig. 91

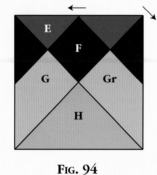

Fig. 92

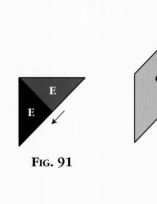

Fig. 93

Fig. 94

Block 2 Assembly

1. Sew a black E triangle to a red E triangle as shown in figure 91. Make one unit.

2. Join a striped G piece, black F square, and red E triangle, as shown in figure 92. Make one unit.

3. Join a yellow H triangle, striped G reversed piece, and black E triangle (fig. 93). Make one unit.

4. Sew the units together to complete a block (fig. 94). Make 84 of block 2.

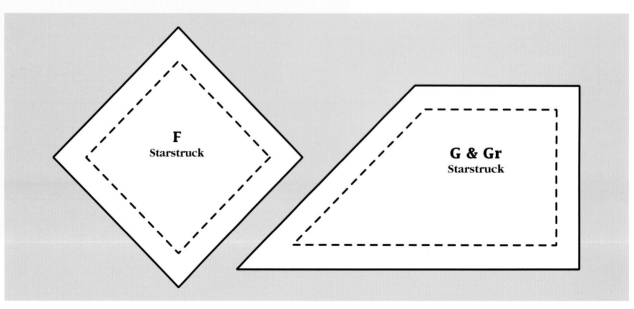

F
Starstruck

G & Gr
Starstruck

Border Cutting

Border lengths include 2½" extra for insurance and seam allowances. Border strips are cut selvage to selvage and need to be pieced.

Fabric	Cutting
Black print	116 pattern F, middle border
Assorted red prints	30 E squares 3¼" x 3¼" ⊠, middle border
Assorted yellow prints	28 E squares 3¼" x 3¼" ⊠, middle border
Yellow print	4 strips 2½" x 58½", inner border
Red print	4 strips 2½" x 66½", outer border

Quilt Assembly

1. Make 13 rows of 13 blocks each, alternating block 1 and block 2 in a checkerboard pattern (fig. 95, page 88). Take care that the star blocks are arranged according to their background colors and that the block 2s are rotated to reveal the pattern.

2. To assemble the pieced border, join a red E triangle, black F square, and yellow E triangle (fig. 96, page 88). Make 112 units, 28 for each side of the quilt.

3. Join two red E triangles and a black F square (fig. 97, page 88). Make four. Use these units at one end of each border strip.

4. Join the units from steps 2 and 3 to make four pieced border strips.

5. For each pieced border strips, sew a yellow inner border to the yellow side and a red outer border to the red side. Sew the combined borders to the quilt and miter the corners.

Finishing

1. Layer, then quilt as desired.

The author covered the entire quilt in hand echo quilting, with lines spaced ⅝" apart. The design extends into the pieced border.

2. Bind with double-fold, straight-grain binding.

3. Sign and date your quilt.

FIG. 95

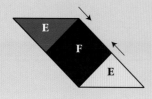

FIG. 96

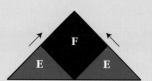

FIG. 97

Tempo

Quilt size: 36" x 36"

Block size: 4"

Fabric Requirements

Yardage is based on 40" wide fabric.

Fabric	Amount
Gold print	½ yd
Rust print	⅝ yd
Black print 1	⅜ yd
Black print 2	⅝ yd
Stripe	178 running inches by 2" wide. See Striped Fabric, page 19, for determining yardage.
Backing	2⅜ yd (2 panels 21" x 40")
Batting	40" x 40"
Binding	⅜ yd (4 strips 2½" x 40")

Making Blocks

Patterns are on page 93.

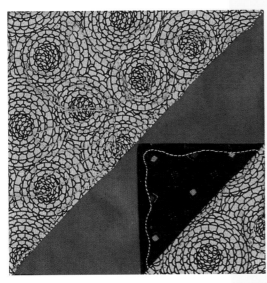

BLOCK 1

BLOCK 2

TEMPO, *by the author, machine quilted by Judy Case of Florence, Colorado. This quilt combines two directional blocks. To produce the secondary patterns, the chevron block was rotated, and the other block maintains the same direction throughout the quilt.*

Block 1 Cutting

Fabric	Cutting
Gold print	13 A squares 4⅞" x 4⅞" ◻
	13 B squares 2⅞" x 2⅞" ◻
Rust print	25 B squares 2⅞" x 2⅞" ◻
Black print 1	13 B squares 2⅞" x 2⅞" ◻

Block 1 Assembly

1. Use a gold B square and a black print 1 B square to make two half-square units (fig. 98). Make 25 units.

2. Sew two rust B triangles to the black side of the half-square unit (fig. 99). Make 25 units.

3. Sew a gold A triangle to a unit from step two to complete the block (fig. 100). Make 25 of block 1.

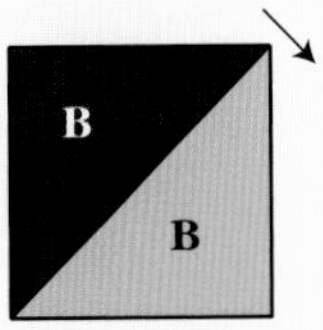

FIG. 98

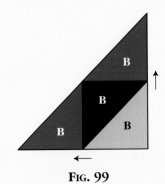

FIG. 99

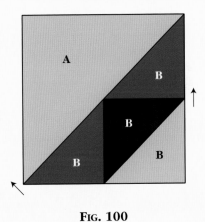

FIG. 100

Block 2 Cutting

Fabric	Cutting
Black print 1	24 B squares 2⅞" x 2⅞" ◻
Black print 2	6 D squares 5¼" x 5¼" ⊠
Stripe	24 pattern C
	24 pattern C reversed

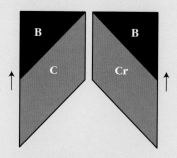

FIG. 101

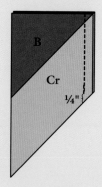

FIG. 102

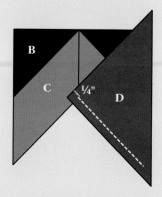

FIG. 103

Block 2 Assembly

1. Sew a black print 1 B triangle to each C and C reversed piece (fig. 101). Make 24 of each unit.

2. Sew the units together in pairs, as shown in figure 102, beginning at the top and stopping ¼" from the bottom to allow for a set-in seam. Backstitch to secure the seam.

3. Sew one short side of a black print 2 D triangle to the inner edge of the B/Cr unit, stopping ¼" from the inner point and backstitching to secure (fig. 103).

4. Pivot the D triangle to sew it to the inner edge of the B/C unit to complete the set-in point (fig. 104). Make 24 of block 2.

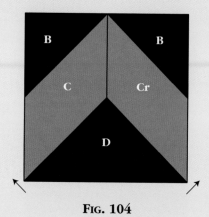

FIG. 104

Border Cutting

Border lengths include 2½" extra for insurance and seam allowances. Border strips are cut selvage to selvage.

Fabric	Cutting
Rust print	2 strips 2½" x 30½", side inner borders
	2 strips 2½" x 34½", top and bottom inner borders
Black print 2	2 strips 2½" x 34½", side outer borders
	2 strips 2½" x 38½", top and bottom outer borders

Quilt Assembly

1. Make seven rows of seven blocks each, alternating block 1 and block 2 in a checkerboard pattern (fig. 105, page 94). Take care that directional block 2 is rotated correctly to reveal the pattern.

2. Sew the 30½" rust borders to the sides of the quilt. Sew the 34½" rust borders to the top and bottom. Add the black print 2 outer borders in the same way.

Finishing

1. Layer, then quilt as desired.

The author's quilt is machine quilted. The overall design includes sunflowers and wavy accent lines.

2. Bind with double-fold, straight-grain binding.

3. Sign and date your quilt.

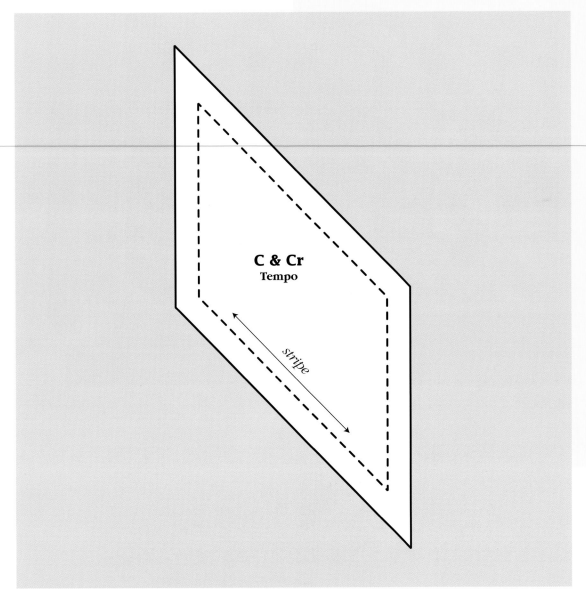

C & Cr
Tempo

stripe

FIG. 105

• **TRADITIONAL Two Block Quilts** • Sally Saulmon

World Without End

QUILT SIZE: 36" x 36"

BLOCK SIZE: 6"

Fabric Requirements

Yardage is based on 40" wide fabric.

Fabric	Amount
Brown stripe	130 running inches by 2½" wide. See Striped Fabric, page 19, for determining yardage.
Assorted beige prints	½ yd total
Assorted gold prints	½ yd total
Assorted red prints	⅝ yd total
Assorted brown prints	⅝ yd total
Assorted rust prints	¼ yd total
Assorted black prints	¼ yd total
Brown print	⅝ yd. Extra yardage will be needed if border is fussy cut.
Backing	2⅜ yd (2 panels 21" x 40")
Batting	40" x 40"
Binding	⅜ yd (4 strips 2½" x 40")

Making Blocks

Patterns are on pages 101-102.

BLOCK 1

BLOCK 2

WORLD WITHOUT END, *by the author. Combining the 30-degree angle in block 1 and the 45-degree angle in block 2 gives the illusion of circles from straight lines.*

Fabric	Cutting
Brown stripe	52 D squares 2½" x 2½"
Assorted beige prints	26 pattern B
Assorted gold prints	26 pattern B
Assorted red prints	9 A squares 2½" x 2½"
	26 pattern C
	26 pattern C reversed
Assorted brown prints	4 A squares 2½" x 2½"
	26 pattern C
	26 pattern C reversed

Block 1 Assembly

1. Sew a red C triangle and a red C reversed triangle to a gold B triangle (fig. 106). Repeat, using brown C and C reversed triangles and a beige B triangle. Make two of each unit.

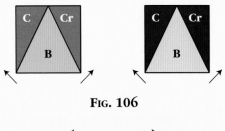

FIG. 106

2. Sew a striped D square to each side of a gold/red unit (fig. 107). Make two of these.

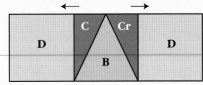

FIG. 107

3. Sew a beige/brown unit to each side of a red or a brown A square (fig. 108). Make one of these.

4. Join the units to complete the block (fig. 109). Make nine of block 1 with a red A square and four with a brown A square.

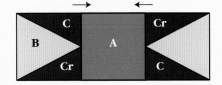

FIG. 108

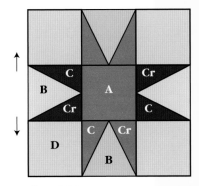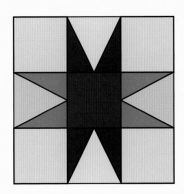

FIG. 109

Fabric	Cutting
Assorted beige prints	12 E squares 2⅞" x 2⅞" 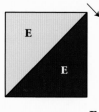
	6 F squares 3¼" x 3¼"
Assorted gold prints	12 E squares 2⅞" x 2⅞"
	6 F squares 3¼" x 3¼"
Assorted red prints	6 A squares 2½" x 2½"
	12 E squares 2⅞" x 2⅞"
	6 F squares 3¼" x 3¼"
Assorted brown prints	6 A squares 2½" x 2½"
	12 E squares 2⅞" x 2⅞"
	6 F squares 3¼" x 3¼"
Assorted rust prints	12 E squares 2⅞" x 2⅞"
Assorted black prints	12 E squares 2⅞" x 2⅞"

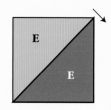

FIG. 110

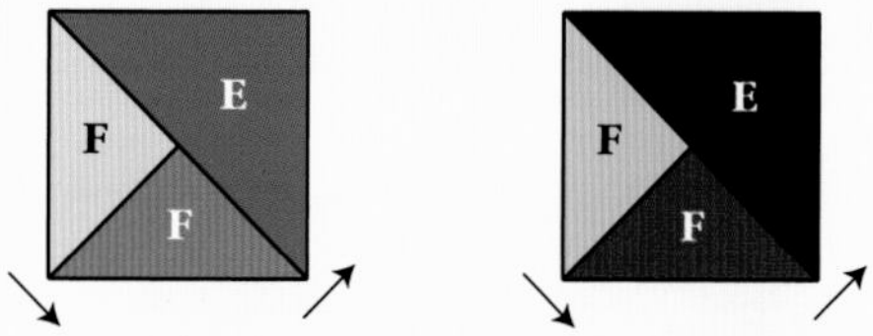

FIG. 111

FIG. 112

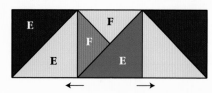

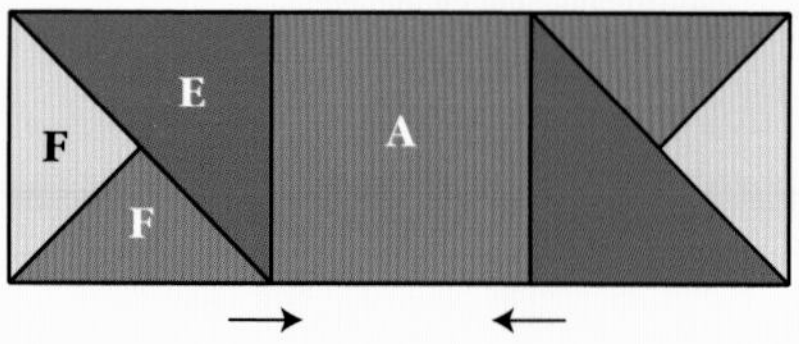

FIG. 113

Block 2 Assembly

1. Use a beige E square and a brown E square to make four half-square units. Also make four half-square units in red and gold (fig. 110).

2. Sew a red F triangle to a beige F triangle along the short edge. Add a rust E triangle. Make four tri-color units. In the same manner, make four tri-color units in brown, gold, and black (fig. 111).

3. Join two half-square units and a tri-color unit as shown in figure 112. Make two of these rows.

4. Join a tri-color unit to each side of a red A square as shown in figure 113. Make one row.

5. Complete the red and rust star block 2 by sewing the rows together.

6. Make block 2 in the following color combinations (fig. 114):

6 with a red (A & F) and rust (E) star, beige background (E & F), and brown corner triangles (E)

6 with a brown (A & F) and black (E) star, gold background (E & F), and red corner triangles (E)

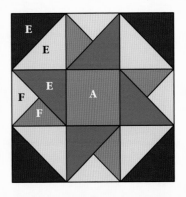

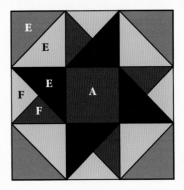

FIG. 114

Border Cutting

Fabric	Cutting
Brown print	4 pattern G
	4 pattern H
	4 pattern H reversed
Assorted beige prints	4 pattern B
Assorted gold prints	4 pattern B

Quilt Assembly

1. Make five rows of five blocks, arranging blocks 1 and 2 in a checkerboard pattern (fig. 115, page 100). Rotate block 1 to create the pattern.

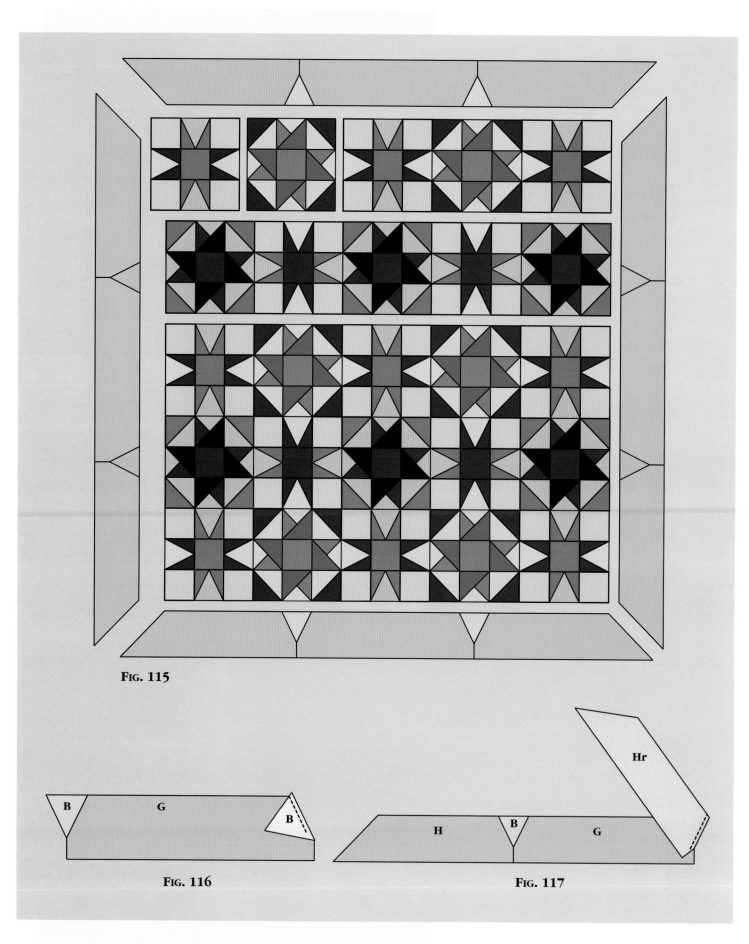

FIG. 115

FIG. 116

FIG. 117

2. For the border strips, sew a beige B triangle to each end of a G piece, stopping ¼" from the points to allow for a set-in seam (fig. 116). Backstitch to secure the seam.

3. Add H and H reversed pieces to each B/G/B unit (fig 117). Be sure to stop sewing ¼" from the B point for the set-in seam. Backstitch.

4. Finish the seams at the B triangles. Make two border units with beige B triangles and two units with gold triangles.

5. Sew the four borders to the quilt, matching the gold B triangles to the gold background blocks and the beige B triangles to the beige background blocks. Miter the corners.

Finishing

1. Layer, then quilt as desired.

For the author's quilt, echo hand quilting, spaced ⅝" apart, is accented with in-the-ditch quilting. The quilting design in the border follows the fabric pattern.

2. Bind with double-fold, straight-grain binding.

3. Sign and date your quilt.

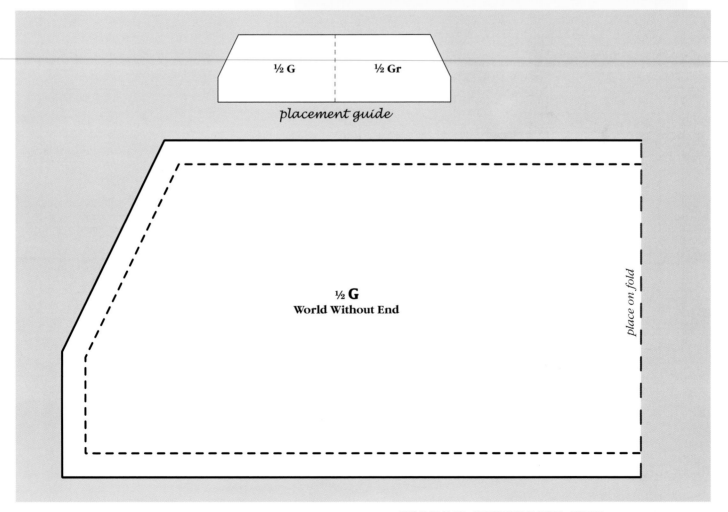

½ G   ½ Gr

placement guide

½ **G**
World Without End

place on fold

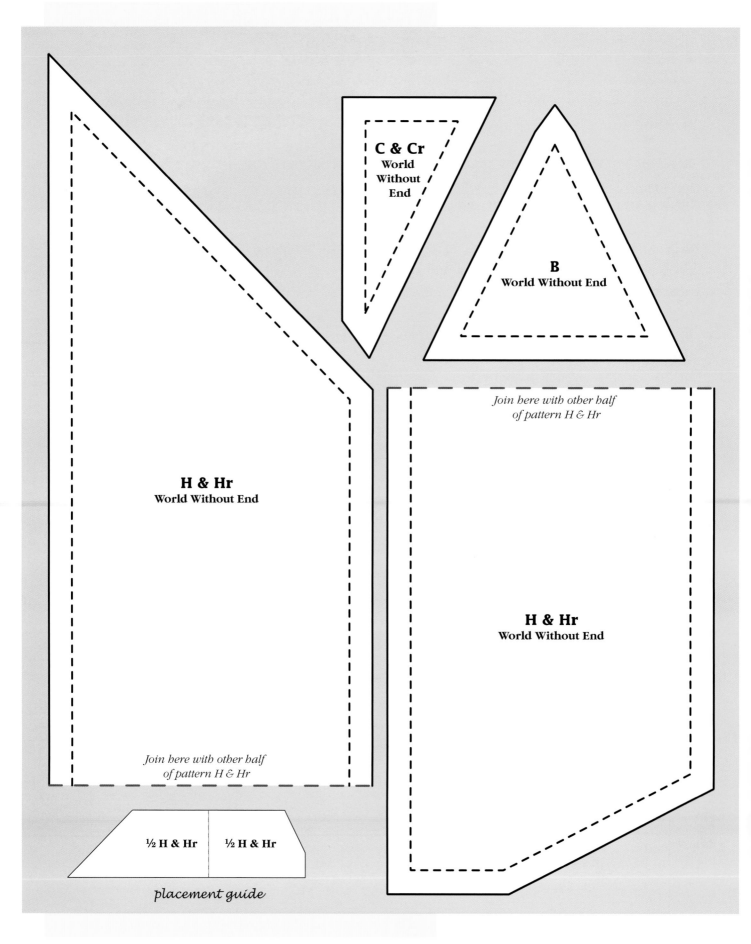

C & Cr
World
Without
End

B
World Without End

H & Hr
World Without End

*Join here with other half
of pattern H & Hr*

H & Hr
World Without End

*Join here with other half
of pattern H & Hr*

½ H & Hr | ½ H & Hr

placement guide

• **TRADITIONAL Two Block Quilts** • Sally Saulmon

Xanadu

QUILT SIZE: 31½" x 31½"
BLOCK SIZE: 6"

Fabric Requirements

Yardage is based on 40" wide fabric.

Fabric	Amount
Yellow print	½ yd
Teal print	½ yd
Green print	¼ yd
Orange print	½ yd
Gold print	¼ yd
Blue-green print	⅞ yd. Buy extra yardage if D or H patches are fussy cut.
Backing	1⅛ yd (1 panel 36" x 36")
Batting	36" x 36"
Binding	⅜ yd (4 strips 2½" x 40")

Making Blocks

Patterns are on page 110.

BLOCK 1

BLOCK 2

BLOCK 3

XANADU, *by the author. This quilt is a combination of three blocks set on point, with pieced setting triangles.*

Block 1 Cutting

Fabric	Cutting
Yellow print	5 C squares 5¼" x 5¼" ⊠
Teal print	20 pattern B
Green print	5 pattern A

Block 1 Assembly

1. Sew a yellow C triangle to each side of a teal B piece (fig. 118). Make two units.

2. Sew a teal B to each side of a green A square (fig. 119).

3. Join the units to complete the block (fig. 120). Make five of block 1.

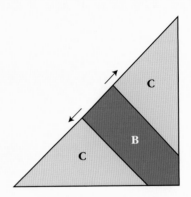

FIG. 118

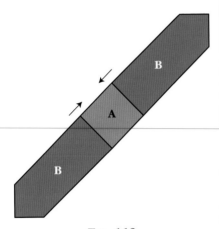

FIG. 119

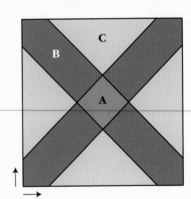

FIG. 120

Block 2 Cutting

Fabric	Cutting
Yellow print	4 E squares 3¼" x 3¼" ⊠
	32 G squares 1½" x 1½" ◨
Teal print	16 F squares 2½" x 2½"
Orange print	8 E squares 3¼" x 3¼" ⊠
Blue-green print	4 pattern D

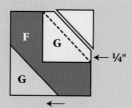

FIG. 121

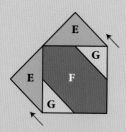

FIG. 122

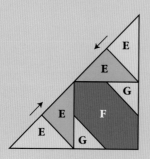

FIG. 123

Block 2 Assembly

1. Use the corner-square technique to add a yellow G square to two opposite corners of a teal F square (fig. 121). Make four units.

2. Sew an orange E triangle to adjacent sides of an F/G unit (fig. 122). Make four of these.

3. Sew two yellow E triangles to two of the E/F/G units as shown in figure 123.

4. Sew two E/F/G units to opposite sides of a blue-green D square (fig. 124).

5. Join the units to complete a block (fig. 125). Make four of block 2.

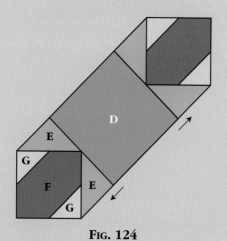

FIG. 124

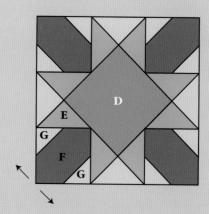

FIG. 125

Fabric	Cutting
Gold print	8 I squares 3⅞" x 3⅞" 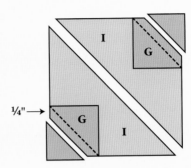
Green print	16 G squares 1½" x 1½"
Blue-green print	4 H squares 4¾" x 4¾"

Block 3 Assembly

1. Use the corner-square technique to add a green G square to two opposite corners of a gold I square. Cut the square in half diagonally to obtain two half-square units (fig. 126). Make four units.

2. Sew a unit to all four sides of a blue-green H square to complete the block (fig. 127). Make four of block 3.

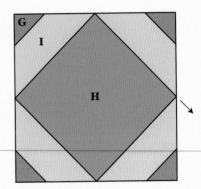

FIG. 126

FIG. 127

Fabric	Cutting
Orange print	4 L squares 2⅞" x 2⅞"
	4 M squares 5⅞" x 5⅞"
Teal print	8 pattern J
	8 pattern K
Green print	8 G squares 1½" x 1½"

Setting Triangle Assembly

1. For the corner setting triangles, sew a teal K piece to an orange L triangle. Sew two of these together as shown in figure 128. Make four corner triangles.

2. For the side setting triangles, sew a teal J piece to an orange M triangle. Use the corner-square technique to add a G square on the point of the orange M triangle (fig. 129). Make eight side triangles.

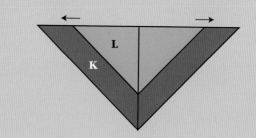

FIG. 128

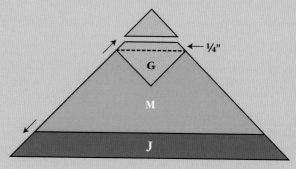

FIG. 129

Border Cutting

Border lengths include 2½" extra for insurance and seam allowances. Border strips are cut selvage to selvage.

Fabric	Cutting
Blue-green print	2 strips 3½" x 28", side borders
	2 strips 3½" x 34", top and bottom borders

Quilt Assembly

1. Arrange the blocks on point, as shown on the quilt layout (fig 130). Add the corner and side setting triangles as shown.

2. Sew the two blue-green side border strips to the quilt sides. Then add the top and bottom blue green borders.

Finishing

1. Layer, then quilt as desired.

In this quilt, the blocks and setting triangles are hand quilted in an echo pattern spaced ⅝" apart and accented with in-the-ditch quilting. The quilting in the medallions and outside border follow the parrot and leaf motifs of the fabric.

2. Bind with double-fold, straight-grain binding.

3. Sign and date your quilt.

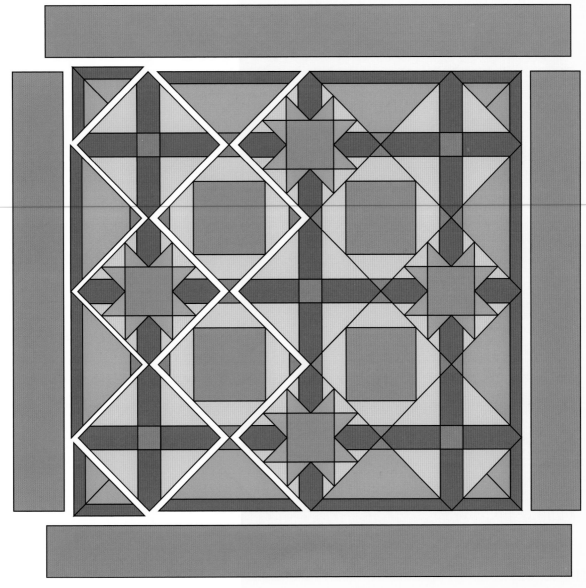

FIG. 130

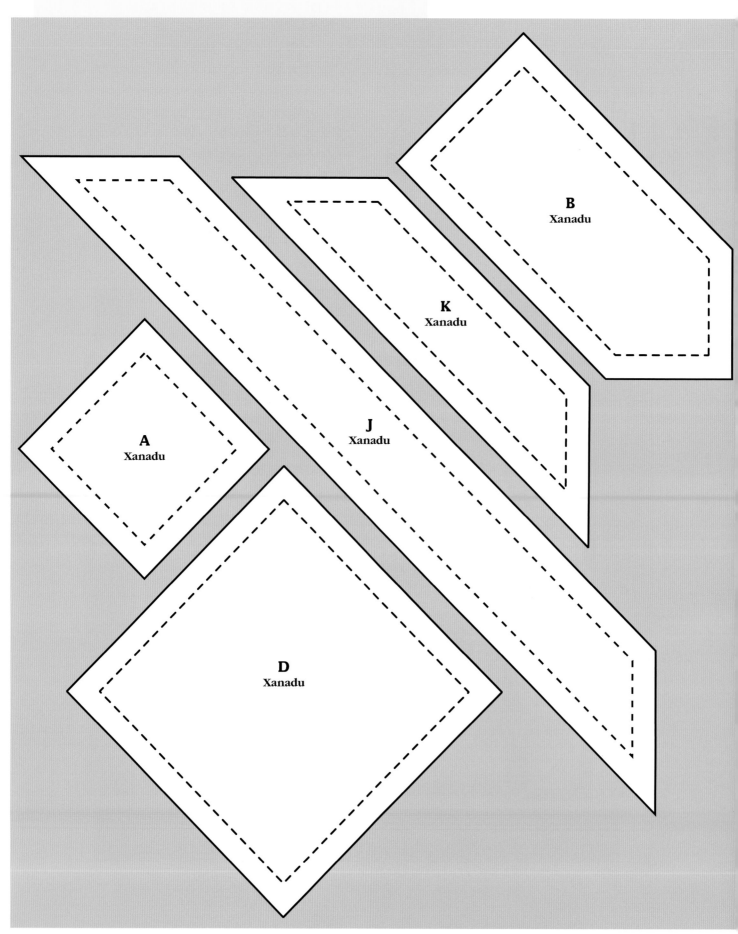

B
Xanadu

K
Xanadu

A
Xanadu

J
Xanadu

D
Xanadu

About the Author

Sally Saulmon learned to quilt from her grandmothers at an early age. They were primarily utility quilters, making simple geometric quilts and an occasional embroidered quilt. The only design advice she received from them was: "Most quilts need a little red in them!"

From this basic beginning, and with her interest in mathematics, Sally began to experiment with the interaction of geometric shapes. Wanting to bring a contemporary edge to her very traditional quilts, in 1982, Sally began exploring two-block quilt designs. She became enchanted with the way two or more blocks come together to produce surprising new patterns. Many of her two-block quilts have now been exhibited and published, and several have won recognition.

In 1988, she began teaching her concepts for two-block quilt design. She also enjoys teaching classes on signature quilts and on using striped fabric effectively in quilts. Having taught quiltmaking for 30 years, Sally brings a wealth of experience to her students.

Beyond the sewing room, Sally's life includes her husband, Bob, a retired engineer, and their two grown children. Their son, Michael, is a math and science teacher, and daughter Jennifer and her family live close by. Sally's full-time job is providing daycare for her two grandchildren.

Sally is also the author of *Keepsake Signature Quilts,* published by the American Quilter's Society in 2003.

Other AQS books

This is only a small selection of the books available from the American Quilter's Society. AQS books are known worldwide for timely topics, clear writing, beautiful color photos, and accurate illustrations and patterns. The following books are available from your local bookseller, quilt shop, or public library.

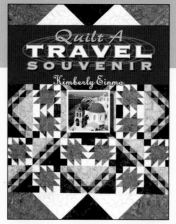

#6805   us$22.95

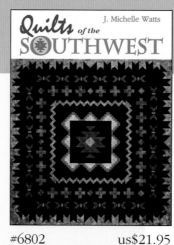

#6802   us$21.95

#6677   us$21.95

#6293   us$24.95

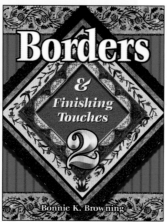

#6804   us$22.95

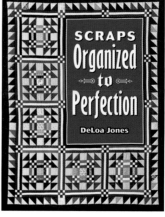

#6007   us$22.95

#6515   us$19.95

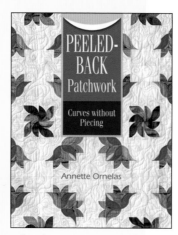

#6516   us$21.95

#6412   us$21.95

Look for these books nationally.
Call or **Visit** our Web site at

1-800-626-5420
www.AmericanQuilter.com